When The Ark Turns Aside

The Glory Shall Return

DR. DONALD A. WRIGHT

"I've known Bishop Donald Wright for a long time, and the truth is he's a brilliant voice. When the Ark Turns Aside is a continuation of that brilliance. I pray as you read this, your mind and your spirit will be stretched to new and exciting places. Enjoy the adventure."

-Dr. John E. Guns, Dean,
Samuel Dewitt Proctor School of Theology,
Virginia Union University

"As I read this manuscript, I was captured by the wisdom and revelation given to Bishop Donald Wright by God. The quickening of the Holy Spirit truly captured me. To think how our One and Only True Living God reveals Himself to mankind. My prayer for all who reads this book is that you would have the same like kind experience that I have had. So much so that you will want to sow this book as a seed to someone else."

- Bishop Andrew Merritt, Senior Pastor,
Straight Gate International Church

"The people of God desperately need the presence of God. In When The Ark Turns Aside, Bishop Donald Wright succinctly shows the path to the Lord's presence and principles that can release His power in today's church."

-Archbishop Robert J. Rochford,
Chief Prelate, Dunamis Covenant Connection
Senior Pastor, New Life Cathedral

Acknowledgements

To my wife Nakia, who believes that I can do the
impossible even when it's difficult.

To my church family, The Gathering at Forestville
who supported me in this effort.

To Tasheka L. Green, who helped to make this
work possible, thank you.

Published by Dr. Donald A. Wright August 2021

Address: 7819 Parston Drive Forestville, MD 20747
Website: https://www.thegaf.net
Email: info@thegaf.net
Social Media: @Theegafmd

First Edition: August 2021

Library of Congress Cataloging in Publication Data
Names: Wright, Donald A. D.D., D.Min., Ph.D.
Title: When the Ark Has Turned Aside: The Return of His Glory
Description: First Edition. | Forestville, Maryland
 Includes bibliographical references.
Identifiers: LLCN 20221912443 | ISBN: 978-0-578-93988-9 (large print)

Subjects: Religious-Christianity

Scripture quotations are from the Holy Bible, God's Word Translation (GW), King James Version, (KJV), The Message (MSG), New International Version (NIV), and New Living Translation (NLT).

Printed in the United States of America

Dedication

As every father I love all my children, and as I
passionately reached into my heart for this work, I
wish to honor Derrick.
Always fighting for those counted out, caring for
family, seeking the equal better for all;
son, never stop.

Contents

Introduction

I will always be indebted to God's grace that was responsible for birthing a drive to answer a few questions as it concerned just some of the unsearchable riches of God. In my quest to know more and be a better student of the text, I discovered in some cases and rediscovered in others that his grace always leads you to his order. In his righteousness, through his love, we find he clearly reveals his order to manifest his plans. While we're in that seeking time, we must operate with great humility to be led by his spirit to the illumination that we so desire. Without that spirit of humility, we will constantly entertain doubt and fall on the road of misdirection that can be birthed by a misguided imagination concerning eternal things. We will be well served to remember the ways of God are perfect. Any changes or substitutions on our part creates an area of imperfection that would be misleading and consequential. While quick answers and people-pleasing ideas may be self-serving and ego nurturing, they hardly impress or measure up to the immutable plan that was before the foundation of the world. With the needs of this world groaning for help and aid from the assigned of God, we would do well to reexamine the text as many before us. These signs shall follow them that believe was a promise given, and yet, the world is in desperate need of the plans and promises of its creator. This small work is only an attempt to awaken the greatness in you, that men would see good works and glorify our Father.

Foreword

Over the years, I have been privileged to call Donald Wright my friend. We met while we were both pioneering and pastoring churches in North Carolina. I am always moved by his love for Jesus, the Scriptures, the Church, and the prophetic sense of the direction Jesus is taking the Church. Amid a season of uncertainty and the kinds of seismic upheavals that we are all experiencing in the current hour, I asked Donald what he was seeing and sensing. He began to pour from his heart and share about how the ark has turned aside.

Donald immediately began to reflect on that moment in Israel's history during the days of Saul, Israel did not really seek the Lord, and it was in that season when the ark of God had been taken captive by the Philistines.

As he began to reflect on that moment in history, Donald was drawn to the scriptures. He referenced that it was not until Yahweh, who allowed himself to be taken captive in symbolic fashion by the Ark being lost in battle and placed in the house of Dagon, the Philistine god, that God in that place of exile in the Temple of Dagon, began to tear down every high thing in Philistia that had exalted itself above the knowledge of God.

Remember that old saying, "God is God all by himself!" It is really appropriate here.

Donald continued to talk about how the God of Abraham, Isaac, and Jacob dealt a humiliating death blow to Dagon in Dagon's own house. If that wasn't enough, Yahweh sent plagues throughout the Philistine culture that were carried by rodents. In addition, whatever was impacting their water, and their food affected their digestive tracts. As a result, all the people began to have severe hemorrhoidal issues that were quite painful. It is evident that there are consequences for those who don't know how to interact with the One True God.

The fact that Donald brought to life is that the Philistines were desperate to have life get back to normal because the God of the Israelites was wreaking havoc on their culture, their god, and their beliefs. They couldn't afford to lose what they had built into the consciousness of their people, even though the priests and leaders realized in the very center of the Temple of Dagon that Dagon was no match for Yahweh. Had they repented, the story might have ended a different way. Nevertheless, they wanted to appease the wrath of Yahweh, and so they made golden mice and golden hemorrhoids to be given as a gift to Yahweh. In addition, they built a cart and placed two female milking cows in harness to tow the Ark in hopes that those milk cows would leave their young (quite unusual) and travel a path that would bring the Ark back to the Israelites. This brought Donald to a point in sharing where the current culture is and how strikingly similar it may be to that little piece of history from the nation of Israel.

Donald then noted that Yahweh was clearly guiding the milk cows to head back through the territory Joshua had already conquered that was lost in battle to the Philistines. In the wheat fields of Beth-Shemesh, during the heat and drought of the summer, at a certain point, the laborers in the fields heard the lowing of female cows and the sound of wheels moving. They saw that the Ark was being transported back into the hands of the Israelites. Yahweh was no longer held captive, and He emerged victorious, even without the help of the army of Israel. The laborers shouted a great shout.

If you recall the story, they brought the ark to Abinadab, who some argue was a Levite, and it was in his hands and under his care for twenty years. In fact, during the reign of Saul, the Ark wasn't even given a second thought. This was something else Donald expressed was needed to be understood in terms of the signs of our times. So, it sat in Abinadab's house, virtually disregarded. Things got to a place in Israel, where the physical piece of furniture that symbolized the abiding presence of God was totally inconsequential. It wasn't even a thought on Saul's mind, and perhaps not even on the minds of the people. Donald was commenting on how it is one thing for the Philistines not to know what to do with the God of Abraham, Isaac, and Jacob. It is quite another for the people of God not to know what to do. The greater responsibility fell on the people of God and indeed fall today on the Church.

David was finally made king. He wanted all things to be put in their appropriate place and wanted the nation to seek the Lord again. In the economy of Moses, to seek the Lord required understanding that they had to follow the cloud of glory that sat over the Ark of the Covenant, from the beginning of their desert journey to the border of the Land of Canaan. When David decided that it was time to bring the Ark of God "home" where it belonged, he planned a great parade.

The festival day arrived, and yet the sons of Israel copied the Philistines and built a new cart for the ark and hitched up two oxen to it, and Abinadab, who, if he was a Levite, should have known that God never commanded the Ark to be placed on a cart and driven. Donald was very precise in addressing how much the people of God today had forgotten about the protocol of the Kingdom of Heaven. As the drama played out, Donald was emphatic about how Uzzah and Ahio "drove" the cart, as if God's presence could be "driven." Then he noted that they got to a bump in the road, the Ark teeter-tottered, and Uzzah and Ahio tried to steady the Ark with their hands. We know what happened then. At that point, it didn't end well.

Donald began to share from that point his convictions about where we are in this season and history and where we need to be if we are to be faithful to the call of God. What you have in your hands is an in-depth outpour of Donald's heart. This book you are about to read takes you on a journey with the Ark of God to its ultimate resting place. I am grateful that Donald took the time to share his heart by putting what was in his heart in print. I pray it gets a wide reading as I believe it deserves one.

I am grateful for Donald's willingness to fashion what you hold in your hands. Happy Reading!

Dr. Mark J. Chironna
Church On The Living Edge
Mark Chironna Ministries
Longwood, Florida

Chapter 1
What Should We Know

It wasn't long ago I was chatting with a good brother, and the conversation came up about grace. He shared that his opinion was we were living in the dispensation of grace. I could not help but pause while thinking of God's constant goodness and I responded grace is no new thing for us in this time, but His unmerited love and favor has always been on display. It is easy to see even in the beginning, he spoke everything into existence. However, when it came to man, he formed them and then blew into them. He didn't speak as he did to the animals or any land development. It was the image of him. This self-image was made with love and pride. It was very good! He was made a living soul (1 Corinthians 15:45). So involved and invested in man, he made visits daily to inquire and to fellowship. Dominion and fellowship would be the manifested desire of our loving God to Adam, to be allowed daily exchanges and given authority of a creation he didn't work for. What a gift, no wonder it was paradise. Not to belabor a point early, but it's not hard to see the wonderment of the psalmist *"What is man, that thou art mindful of him? And the son of man, that thou visitest him? For thou hast made him a little lower than the angels, And hast crowned him with glory and honor. Thou madest him to have dominion over the works of thy hands; thou hast put all things under his feet"* (Psalm 8:4-6 KJV). When the satan appeared as a serpent, his misleading rhetoric caused Adam to sin. Adam's glory was removed, Eve inherited the penalty of her disobedience, and the serpent was made to crawl. It didn't stop there; all of the creation of Hashem was subject to the choice of he, who was given dominion. Even to this day, it groans (Romans 8:22). At first glance, one would think the act of disobedience cancelled the hope for all; however, His mercy endures forever. On many occasions when grace has been violated, mercy responds to restore the right path for the fulfillment of God's plan. It's important to note that neither the love of God nor the plan of God was made dim by the disappointing fall of Adam. All throughout the book of Genesis, we find the continuity of God's plans to Tabernacle or dwell with his people. There is an intentional, traceable, definitive line of his love from generation to generation. We have visited many times the book of Genesis to consult with Abraham about the level of faith we should walk in; however, there is also an expression of the father assigned to Abraham as it relates to the Kingdom of God. With Abraham, it is revealed that God's desire to fellowship with men has seemingly increased exponentially. He informs the Patriarch, *"And I will make of thee a great nation"* (Genesis 12:2). With good reason and the natural order of influence, we examine the lives of Abraham, Isaac, and Jacob. However, it is not until Joseph comes on the scene, and with all the tragedies of his life, we find this great-grandson of Abraham elevated to 2nd in command in a heathen nation.

Only after the life of Joseph do we recognize that Israel has grown and flourished to become the nation that was spoken of to the Prophet and patriarch Abraham.

We are introduced to a people who were proud and clear about the declaration of Abraham as he went up the mountain with his son Isaac to worship and offer a sacrifice, along with his confession that he would come back down the mountain and his son would be whole.

"And Abraham said unto his young men, abide ye here with the ass; and I and the lad will go yonder and worship, and come again to you" (Genesis 22:5 KJV). Yet, the superior strength and the greed of men forced the thumb of slavery onto the chosen people of God who worked and fulfilled some of the harshest demands of their time. It doesn't go unnoticed that the Egyptians were polytheistic, meaning they regularly answered to more than one God. It's a wise study to search why the Lord ordered 10 plagues on the Egyptians; however, Moses gave instruction to the children of Israel, and they were victorious in all. Egypt spoke of the world. Full of paganism and materialism, it's affected upon the character and spirituality of God's people was generally mostly negative. Egypt does not represent spiritual life but spiritual death.

There were, however, exceptions when Israel's being in Egypt did not reflect disobedience. One case was that of Jacob and his family going to Egypt in Joseph's time. Another was when Joseph and Mary in the New Testament were ordered to take the Christ child to Egypt for several years for protection from Herod (Matthew 2:13-15). Carnality would like to make the exception the rule, but spiritual minds know better and will not go to Egypt unless there is a clear, unmistakable command from God. Such was the case in Joseph and Mary taking the Christ child.

"And the children of Israel were fruitful, an increased abundantly, and multiplied, and waxed exceedingly mighty; and the land was filled with them" (Exodus 1:7 KJV). The productivity of Israel in Egypt was the fulfillment of a promise which God had given Jacob when Jacob and his family were moving to Egypt. God promised Jacob "and I will there make of thee a great nation" (Genesis 46:3). This would fall directly in line with the promise that he made to Abraham. The fulfillment of this promise gives us good lessons about the fulfillment of all divine promises. "***There***" was the place of fulfillment. "***There***" in Jacob's case, meant Egypt. God's promise specified the place for its fulfillment. Had Jacob in his family not abode in Egypt as instructed, they would have missed the blessing of this fulfillment.

Not every place is the divinely appointed place of blessing. It is, therefore, very important that we be in the particular place where God said the blessing would be if we expected to receive the promised blessing. As an example, the Prophet Jeremiah was instructed to go to the Potter's house to hear from God. Jeremiah was told, *"there"* I will cause thee to hear my words (Jeremiah 18:1). Had Jeremiah not gone to the Potter's house as instructed; he would not have received the blessing of hearing God's word.

Those who complain they are coming up short on the promise of the blessings of God are often those who are not careful about being *"there"* in the place of blessings. Promises are not apart from responsibilities. One of the great responsibilities is to be *"there"* in the appointed place of blessing. For those who have difficulty with knowing where *"there"* is, and many do, it's simply where His spirit ordered our presence. As an example, *"there"* will be church on Sunday morning and not in other places.

"There" may not be where we necessarily want to be. But wherever God's *"there"* is, is where the promised blessing will meet us, and it is, therefore, the best place for us to be. We need to be *"there,"* no matter what our feelings say. I've often believed the safest place on the earth is the center of God's will!

The Israelites did not maintain a high standard of faith in Egypt. A few did such as the parents of Moses, but a great portion of Israel was polluted spiritually and morally. Joshua even had words of condemnation after they had arrived in

Canaan. *"Put away the gods which your fathers served on the other side of the flood {the Euphrates}, and in Egypt, and serve Ye the Lord"* (Joshua 24:14 KJV). We are also reminded in Ezekiel 20:7 of God's disappointment, *"Cast ye away every man the abominations of his eyes and defile not yourselves with the idols of Egypt"* (Ezekiel 20:7 KJV). Israel not only needed to be taken out of Egypt, but Egypt needed to be taken out of Israel. Unfortunately, Israel was taken out of Egypt much easier and quicker than Egypt was taken out of Israel.

We will soon discover that David suffered from just a few of the same issues. Let's not forget, David was Saul's replacement. When the only example you've ever known was a wicked King that lost favor and anointing, it leaves you no history to follow. But we will examine that in the chapters to come.

The scriptures are full of the divine providence and mercies of God; however, nothing would seem more loving than his rescue of Moses out of the waters that his servant would escape death (Exodus 1:16). Before the foundation of the world, Moses was the choice to be the deliverer of Israel for almighty God. The time could not be more difficult, for the Egyptians were benefiting from the slavery of God's people. This picture is not unique. J. G. Butler reminds us we can write chapters like Exodus 1 about every age of man. When man turns from God and serves his own base passions, he can become like a brute beast in his treatment of his fellow man. Though he is educated, sophisticated, and computerized, he can become a jungle in morals and manners without God. Even as the children of Israel were considered second-class citizens in Egypt, that didn't seem to matter, for they felt that they still prospered under the hand of the oppressor. Egypt had been a land of ease and luxury. Because of that, it encouraged the spiritual and moral decay of their souls. According to Edersheim, Goshen, which is to this day considered the richest province in Egypt would especially provide ease and luxury, for the fertileness of the land and the warm climate prevailed there. Beneath the seductive influences of the Egyptian climate, their character became more relaxed. Abraham's monotheistic teaching began to dim in their eyes. Moral decay usually causes you to submit to the gods that are in front of you. Such was the case with Israel.

The audacity of God to think he could take a man with a history of murder and a mindset that hadn't changed from being in hiding for over 40 years, and that man would faithfully honor his every word is beyond fascinating! But that is exactly what he thought about his choice named Moses. This burning bush introduction has multiple layers to it. The triune God who speaks out to Moses again begins a demonstration with three manifestations. The first, his rod and snake, the second, his hand and leprosy, and the third, water from the Nile River and blood. Just for a moment, I would like to examine the rod.

7

Later it will be used in the great plagues upon Egypt. It's also sometimes called Aaron's rod in a number of these plagues, but it was properly Moses' rod which was placed in Aaron's hands inasmuch as Aaron was acting on behalf of Moses. And of course, it would be used to open the Red Sea for the Israelites (Exodus 14:16), to bring water from the rock (Exodus 17:5), and to give victory over the Amalekite's (Exodus 17:8-13). Moses is told to lay the rod that is in his hand on the ground. The need of courage is demonstrated here in the way Moses was to pick up the snake. Moses was instructed to pick it up by the tail, which is the most dangerous way to pick up a snake. The safest way would have been to grab it by the head so the snake could not bite. This pictures the danger that Moses would enter in confronting Pharaoh and the courage he would need to do his work. But he was successful in picking up the snake here because God was with him. And because God would also be with Moses in Egypt, Moses would be successful in his battle with Pharaoh even though Moses was in a very precarious position when dealing with Pharaoh.

The second miracle with leprosy on his hand was a demonstration of the worst type of leprosy. It could be stated that there should be no confidence in the arm of flesh; however, it demonstrates God's ability to restore a nation full of idolatry with divine favor.

The third miracle God showed Moses was to take the water out of the Nile River and pour it on dry land. The water that he poured out became blood upon the dry land. The message was one of divine judgment. It spoke of retribution just as the previous two miracles spoke of revolt and restoration, respectively. God's retribution for Egypt's ungodly aggression would be clear.

These miracles were credentials and strong proof that Moses was God's man. God still accompanies his servants with proof of the calling. It may not be the same proof in every case, but it will be proof that fits each person's calling. Wise men will recognize these proofs, and the person called will also be recognized of them. Some who professed to have a calling do not have the proof of it in their lives. This is because they are either presuming a call or they are disobedient to a call. Woe be to those who presume a calling that is not their calling. But also, woe be to those who refused to obey the calling. Either situation will bring God's judgment!

Moses continued to be obedient to the plan of God. His strength before Pharaoh proved to be exactly what Jehovah had promised.

So much has been said already about the trip through the Red Sea; this novice has nothing new to add to that particular place in history at this time.

Victory should always be followed by a praise of thanksgiving. Immediately after crossing the Red Sea, they sang a new song, and the people rejoiced at their victory (Revelation 5:9; Psalm 106:12; 2 Samuel 22:1).

However, it didn't take very long for Israel to look past the grace that was extended to them. At the point of promise, the three days Jehovah had spoken of, they arrived at the land of Mara. It was named such because the water was bitter, and the people grumbled against Moses saying, what shall we drink? Right at the place of promise comes grumbling and complaining. *"Many of life's failures are people who did not realize how close they were to success when they gave up" (Thomas Edison).* Moses cried unto the Lord and was shown a log, he threw it into the water, and the water became sweet. Shortly thereafter, the people came to the wilderness of Sin, where they complained about food. The Lord did the impossible and gave them Manna from heaven. I suppose that with food comes thirst. Next Israel's complaint was about water. Moses was then commanded to smite the rock with his rod. As he smote it, water came from the rock. Then came Amalek to fight with Israel. Joshua is commanded to choose men to go out and fight with Amalek. Moses went to the top of the Hill with the staff of God in his hand. Even though Moses' hands grew weary, they took stones and put them under him. Aaron and Hur assisted him in holding up his hands, one on one side, the other on the other side, and the

Lord gave them victory. Jethro, Moses' father-in-law, heard what God had done for Moses and the children of Israel and came out for a visit. As he witnessed the daily counseling of Moses, he offered wise counsel that Moses was to seek help. In seeking help, he would not continue in the self-destructive pattern of wearing himself out with the daily complaints of the people. Little did Moses know that in just a few days, there was another preordained destiny at Sinai. Another encounter with Jehovah on the mountaintop.

When Moses was called by God at the burning bush to be Israel's emancipator, God commanded Moses that "*When thou has brought forth the people out of Egypt, ye shall serve God upon this Mountain*" (Exodus 3:12 KJV). "This Mountain" was the mountain of God, even Horeb (Sinai).

Grace allowed Moses many mountaintop experiences, but it is the first two that we need to speak to us at this point. The first major revelation Moses received from God at Sinai concerned the statutes for Israel. The second revelation concerned the Tabernacle. It is here where we would concern ourselves.

It's worth noting that God had two exceptional meetings with Moses on the mountaintop, each with glorious outcomes. With his finger, he wrote a law that Israel was to obey but constantly broke. He also renewed his desire to TABERNACLE with his chosen people daily and revealed to Moses images and designs of how this temporary dwelling place should be constructed. *"And let them make me a sanctuary, that I may dwell among them"* (Exodus 25:8 KJV). This strategic statement articulates the very heart of God who has chosen to reveal himself to mankind, the benevolent father who has given to his kingly children the honor of searching him out (Proverbs 25:2).

He continues to echo his desire to be with his people throughout the scriptures. *"Behold the Tabernacle of God is with men, he will dwell with them, they should be his people, and God himself shall be with them"* (Revelation 21:3 KJV). The Mosaic Tabernacle in the wilderness was the Old Testament dwelling place of Jehovah, the God of Israel. At rest, it stood in the center of the 12 tribes, facing East. The glory cloud of his Shekinah abode above it throughout their journeys. To the heathen nations near, this simple tent must have appeared a very common edifice rather than the temple or presence of the God of Israel. Thus, there were THREE dimensions to this Divine pattern (the "excellent things" of Proverbs 22:20 literally means "threefold things") the OUTER COURT, the HOLY PLACE, and the MOST HOLY PLACE.

The Tabernacle was called by various names in scripture. The best-known name is "Tabernacle" (Exodus 25:9). Other names by which it was called include "tent" (Exodus 39:33). "Tent of the congregation" (Exodus 39:40), "Tabernacle of the congregation" (Exodus 27:21) "sanctuary" (Exodus 25:8).

"That I may dwell among them" (Exodus 25:8) is the stated purpose of the Tabernacle. He walked with Adam and Eve, visited with Abraham, but here he comes to *dwell* with his chosen. From then to now, he has had a dwelling place on earth. After the Tabernacle, the temple in the land (2 Chronicles 6:3), then the word became flesh, OUR LORD HIMSELF, and tabernacled among us (John 1:14). Next came the church, and this is the present dwelling place of God in the earth.

Moses so valued the presence of God that he did not want to go anywhere without him. And he said, *"My presence will go with you, and I will give you rest."* And he said to him, *"If your presence will not go with me, do not bring us up from here"* (Exodus 33:14-15). Every Christian believer should feel the same. We show our desire to be with God by our attention to our personal prayer, bible study times, and our attendance and worship at church and with God's people.

In this very new imagery of God's throne in the earth given to Moses, it was then known as the Ark of the Covenant. In the assignment of the Tabernacle, it was the first order of business to make the item that represented the throne of God. Often our teachings go from the Outer Court to the Most Holy; however, the reversed is the true order. God's instructions were clear, **His chair is to always be first.** Also, the dimensions of his room were to be 10 by 10 by 10, the same dimensions of perfection in Revelation 21:16. It is the realm of eternal Salvation of Hebrews 5:9.

The Ark of the Covenant represents the enthroned Jesus as King of Kings and the victory of Jesus in Revelation 3:21. So much more can be said about this throne of God that we will cover in chapters to come.

Chapter Two
Called to be Different

It has been the choice of God and his pattern for my life that while all of his word is living, loving, and directional, I usually find myself reviewing something with David or Paul. I've recognized them as my personal heroes. It seems as if their lives speak to me louder than others. It is with the backdrop of God's plan and grace, I wondered in the pasture of curiosity concerning David. How did such a single figure have so many highs and lows, strengths and weaknesses, victories and missteps but always finding himself back at purpose and searching for the heart of the God whom, Ezekiel would later recognize as Jehovah-Shammah, meaning Jehovah is there! We first find this shepherd guy mentioned twice in the book of Ruth. It's one of the greatest gems in holy rite. A beautiful story of recovery after tragedy. Restoration after total disaster and loss. But also, how commitment, acceptance, and change can bring you to a destiny undeserved and favor to be incorporated into blessings reserved for another.

David is the great-grandson of Boaz, the kinsman redeemer of Elimelech, a man who left his inheritance because of famine. Thank God trouble is not permanent! And when Ruth followed her mother-in-law home after the death of both husbands, there was a plan waiting for her she didn't know about. Grace always has a way of finding an opening to bring about God's plan to dwell with His people. *"Many are the plans of a man, but it is the purpose of the LORD that will stand"* (Proverbs 19:21 ESV).

David is officially introduced to us in a time when the nation Israel is jealous of other nations, and they no longer wanted to remain a theocratic nation. They wanted democracy, the ability to pick a king like every other nation. No longer to hear the voice of the prophet and what saith the Lord, but a man they could choose and follow. Oh, chosen people of God, how could you blow it when you had so much going for you?

We are informed that the Prophet Samuel was weeping concerning the desire of the people of God.

It has been said the first six chapters of 1 Samuel connect with the Book of Judges; "every man did that which was right in his own eyes." The Prophet Eli, failed to correct his ambitious and sinful sons, Hophni and Phineas. Israel's uncorrected behavior led them to believe Jehovah would fight for them under any condition. When another attack of the Philistines occurred, the Ark was stolen, Hophni and Phineas died and when Eli heard that Israel was without the glory of the ARK for the first time ever, he fell backwards and broke his neck.

The Prophet Samuel had been mentored by Eli and had learned the voice of Jehovah. Israel's request to have a king had a few moving parts to it. The Prophet Eli is dead, his sons Hophni and Phineas were killed, the ARK and glory are gone, and we are told in first Samuel 8 that *"Samuel's sons didn't follow in his ways."* The people forgot they were a "chosen people" and wanted a king like the rest of the world.

1 Samuel 8:6–9 (KJV): But the thing displeased Samuel when they said, *"Give us a king to judge us. And Samuel prayed unto the Lord. And the Lord said unto Samuel, hearken unto the voice of the people in all that they say unto thee: for they have not rejected thee, but they have rejected me, that I should not reign over them. According to all the works which they have done since the day that I brought them up out of Egypt even unto this day, wherewith they have forsaken me, and served other gods, so do they also unto thee. Now therefore hearken unto their voice: howbeit yet protest solemnly unto them and shew them the manner of the king that shall reign over them."*

Shortly after Samuel was instructed to anoint Saul to be king, it appeared to the natural eye things were going well. It even had the signs the Lord was going to overlook the choices of his people, and things would be well. A few challenges with the military of other nations, but Israel did well. It even seemed that Saul's son Jonathan had favor and grace as he and his armor-bearer won a great victory as they fought 20 giants of the Philistines in the space of a half-acre and prevailed (1 Samuel 14)! However, there came a day when the Lord remembered the promise he made to Moses when the sons of Amalek caused problems with the children of Israel on the way to the promised land.

Exodus 17:14–16 (KJV): *And the Lord said unto Moses, write this for a memorial in a book, and rehearse it in the ears of Joshua: for I will utterly put out the remembrance of Amalek from under heaven. And Moses built an altar and called the name Jehovah-nissi: For he said, Because the Lord hath sworn that the Lord will have war with Amalek from generation to generation.*

Samuel was instructed to send Saul after a promised word the Lord had given to Moses. While men sometimes forget, we are so glad our Heavenly Father remembers ALL his promises to his beloved.

Saul is instructed to destroy all that pertained to Amalek, "*Now go and smite Amalek, and utterly destroy all that they have, and spare them not; but slay both man and woman, infant and suckling, ox and sheep, camel and ass*" (1 Samuel 15:3 KJV).

However, we are at a place where the new king of Israel has produced great disappointment. He had different opinions on what God said which resulted in great penalty. His instructions were clear, total destruction; however, he wasn't strong enough to resist the temptation of power, personal decision, and choice, which resulted in disobedience to God. Saul felt he had a good idea as he fought, but not as God had commanded, not knowing that a good idea is not always a God idea! When Samuel heard of this atrocity, he sharply rebuked the king!

1 Samuel 15:16–23 (KJV): *Then Samuel said unto Saul, Stay, and I will tell thee what the Lord hath said to me this night. And he said unto him, Say on. And Samuel said, when thou wast little in thine own sight, wasn't thou not made the head of the tribes of Israel, and the Lord anointed thee king over Israel? And the Lord sent thee on a journey, and said, Go and utterly destroy the sinners the Amalekites, and fight against them until they be consumed. Wherefore then didst thou not obey the voice of the Lord, but didst fly upon the spoil, and didst evil in the sight of the Lord? And Saul said unto Samuel, Yea, I have obeyed the voice of the Lord, and have gone the way which the Lord sent me, and have brought Agag the king of Amalek, and have utterly destroyed the Amalekites. But the people took of the spoil, sheep and oxen, the chief of the things which should have been utterly destroyed, to sacrifice unto the Lord thy God in Gilgal. And Samuel said, Hath the Lord as great delight in burnt offerings and sacrifices, as in obeying the voice of the Lord? Behold, to obey is better than sacrifice, and to hearken than the fat of rams. For rebellion is as the sin of witchcraft, and*

stubbornness is as iniquity and idolatry. **"Because thou hast rejected the word of the Lord, He hath also rejected thee from being king."**

Perhaps it would have served Saul well had he known the word of the Lord given to Solomon: 1 Chronicles 28:9 (KJV) "*And thou, Solomon my son, know thou the God of thy father, and serve him with a perfect heart and with a willing mind: for the Lord searcheth all hearts, and understandeth all the imaginations of the thoughts: if thou seek him, he will be found of thee; but if thou forsake him, he will cast thee off forever.*"

It is at this point it appears the hope of Israel to be a nation of democracy as others in their region have fallen short. The choice of Saul and the narcissistic approach to being a monarch can be interpreted as nothing short of idolatry. He wanted to be a King that was tall, handsome, and well-received. His own ambition led him to disobey God directly and return with a sacrifice of his own choosing, suggesting to God this is good enough for you, and this is what I want you to have. Neither does it go without notice that he did throw some of the blame when talking with the Prophet Samuel on the people and stated that the people chose to bring these gifts and offer a sacrifice that clearly was not acceptable to God. What a weak thought of a man that's been given power and favor to lead! When things fall short of what Jehovah said, he says the people wanted it. What a disgusting idea that when he's caught, he would think it was ok because the people wanted it. Tragically, he turned on the very people who wanted him to be king, and also gave blame to them for this unwanted sacrifice that he was commanded to destroy.

Samuel was very clear. Not only was stubbornness, iniquity, and idolatry now present, but disobedience and rebellion now ushered in the sin of witchcraft over the nation of Israel. It makes you wonder if this was the door that was opened for Ahab and Jezebel.

While we often journey to our holy inspiration, The Bible, for solutions to our daily problems and uplifting words of inspiration in times of dire needs, this perhaps may be a good space to pause and ask a question, "What would be the level of disappointment that a kind, creative, nurturing Father would feel when his initial desire was love?" One of the questions asked during catechism is, "What is the chief end of man?" Answer, "The chief end of man, is to worship God and to enjoy his pleasures forever!!" I can only imagine the level of disappointment that God would have, never wanting them to be without his wisdom, but considers their request and providing a king. Then the king strays and opens the door as did Adam to other opinions, which led to idolatry when it was his simplest of desires to have a people that he could love and would unconditionally return their love to him. For one of his creations to choose what would be enough of a sacrifice or to willfully disobey his word and or the word of his prophet should be unthinkable. However, as a man thinketh, so is he.

Is this the time to invoke the words of my dearly departed mom by simply saying, what a mess!

We have discovered that on certain occasions, it would seem as if the grace of God has attached to it a measure of elasticity. The wonder factor of His love constantly challenges us to the edge of our human capacity. Being omniscient, Saul's disobedience had no surprises to Jehovah, neither the choices of his people.

The abiding love we experience today has its origin in eternity. God is love and will do anything to prove and share it with us. On occasion, he will get in our way to bring us to his way. "*Many are the plans in the mind of a man, but it is the purpose of the LORD that will stand*" (Proverbs 19:21 ESV).

And it fell on a day. After the great disappointment of Saul, while Samuel was weeping for the destiny of the king, Jehovah spoke and told him to fill his horn with oil, another had been provided in the house of Jesse (1 Samuel 16:1).

The primary purpose of anointing with the holy anointing oil was to sanctify, to set the anointed person or object apart as qodesh, or "Holy" (Exodus 30:29). Originally, the oil was used exclusively for the priests and the Tabernacle articles, but its use was later extended to include kings (1 Samuel 10:1).

The biblical record of the life of David, the greatest King in the history of the nation of Israel, begins with the anointing by the Prophet Samuel to be king and the replacement of Saul.

This was the first of three anointings for David as King of Israel. The other two anointings occurred when he became King at Hebron over part of Israel (the tribe of Judah) in 2 Samuel 2:4, and when he became King over all Israel (2 Samuel 5:3) seven years later. The first anointing occurred when David was still a young person. Our text for this study, especially the part about his shepherd work, would indicate that he was somewhere in his teens, some say between 16 and 18.

To study the first anointing of David as King of Israel, we will consider the conditions for the anointing, the command for the anointing, and the choosing for the anointing.

The anointing of David by Samuel came when the conditions in Israel were very dark, and as such, they underscored the great need for a new King in Israel. Conditions would even get worse before David would actually be seated on the throne of Israel, but God often waits till the situation gets really bad before he brings deliverance. He does this to show the glory of his great power. Bad times did not indicate that God is weak and has lost control of things. Rather, bad times indicate that man is weak and has lost control of things, and man becomes weak through his disobedience. God, however, is always in control. There is no better proof than when things are at their worst; God will step in and provide deliverance and victory.

Given of the distressful conditions in the land when David came on the scene, it is worth mentioning here that the introduction of David in the scripture is like that of the introduction of Samuel in scripture. These two men formed a great contrast to the men they were to replace. Samuel was a great contrast to wicked Eli, whom Samuel replaced as judge. And David was a great contrast to the wicked Saul whom David would replace as King. God's men will always be a great contrast to the evil men of the world. The bleakness of the conditions in Israel at the time of David's anointing is especially seen in the mourning of the Prophet Samuel, the misery of the people, the madness of Saul, and the menace of the Philistines.

Samuel mourned for Saul. When the godly in the land are mourning, conditions in the land are bad. And none were more godly in Israel at this time than the Prophet Samuel. Samuel's mourning for Saul was certainly strong evidence of the need for a new King in Israel and greatly emphasized why it was time for David's anointing.

Samuel had some very good reasons for mourning for Saul. We note the two main reasons why Samuel would mourn for Saul, they were the rebellion of Saul, and the rejection of Saul.

First, the rebellion of Saul began with much promise as Israel's first King. The great victory over the Amorites, who had threatened much harm to the inhabitants of Gilead, showed Saul's compassion for the people of Israel over whom

24

he ruled; and it also showed military courage and skill. It was a very impressive victory. But then, shortly thereafter, things began to go bad for Saul, for he rebelled against God. It started when he would not wait for Samuel to come to Gilgal to make the appointed sacrifice but did the forbidden and made the sacrifice himself. Then later, he rebelled again. This time it was regarding the war with the Amalekites. Saul would not destroy everything that God ordered to be destroyed and so foolishly tried to justify his actions when confronted by Samuel about this rebellion. Scriptures say Saul's rebellion grieved Samuel (1 Samuel 15:11) so much that he cried unto the Lord all night. We need to note that the word grieved here involves more than just mourning. It also involved great vexation and disgust. Samuel was not only sorrowful over Saul's rebellion, but he was also very provoked by Saul's rebellion. Would that all of us would get as upset about rebellion against the Lord, especially when we see it in our own lives.

Second, Saul's rebellion against God led to his rejection from the throne by God. Rebellion against God will always lead to rejection by God. At Gilgal, where Saul did the forbidden by administering the sacrifice, God, through Samuel, gave the first announcement of the rejection of Saul by saying, "*Thy Kingdom shall not continue*" (1 Samuel 13:14). Also, again at Gilgal, God made a second announcement regarding Saul's rejection as King of Israel.

Included in Samuel's rebuke was the pairing of rebellion and demonic activity. It's worth noting that Saul's rebellion was '*as the sin of witchcraft'* (1 Samuel 15:23). This second announcement of rejection was made when Samuel met Saul coming back from the attack of the Amalekites. Through Samuel, God said then, "*Thou has rejected the word of the Lord, and the Lord hath rejected thee from being king over Israel*" (1 Samuel 15:26 KJV). Though Saul replaced Samuel as Israel's ruler, Samuel still obviously had great respect for Saul and had hopes for him. Hence Saul's rejection by God would cause Samuel to greatly mourn.

This rejection of Saul opened the door for David to be King with the throne taken away from Saul and his family (1 Samuel 13:13). The Lord sought him a man after his own heart to be captain over his people (1 Samuel 13:14), and that man was David who was "better than thou" {Saul}. No man is indispensable. Rebel against God, and he will fill your place with someone who is better than you!

God rebuked Samuel for his mourning for Saul. It was not a rebuke for mourning per se, but it was a rebuke for mourning too much. This rebuke is seen in the divine question, "*How long will thou mourn*?" The question is condemning, for God never asks unless sorrow has deepened into an accusation of his providence or tears have blinded us to the duty that ensues. Ezekiel 9 (KJV) says, "*Go through the midst of the city through the midst of Jerusalem and set a mark upon the foreheads of the men that sigh and that cry for all the abominations that be done in the midst thereof."* And the next two verses in Ezekiel say to smite those who do not sigh and cry for the sins of Jerusalem. Samuel was one who sighed and cried for the abominations which were done by Saul in his day. But sorrow, whatever the circumstances, may be carried too far. It may be indulged until it unfits us for duty or darkens our hope in God; it may disturb our peace and weaken our energies; it may be made an occasion where we pause too long and neglect our call to duty. As good a man as Samuel was, he still fell into the snare of excessive lamenting. We can understand why he was mourning, because there were plenty of problems present. But Samuel's problem was that he focused too much on Saul, which only produced despondency and not enough on God which would encourage hope, deliverance, and answers to the present dilemma.

God's love always has a remedy for our mourning. *"Fill thine horn with oil and go."* God gave Samuel an excellent antidote for his sorrow. He gave him work to do, namely, anointing David as King. The true cure for sorrow is the work of the kingdom. Of course, such work must be sanctioned by God. When trouble is the cause of sorrow, we will be a victim of sorrow if we just sit and do nothing. The sad developments will continue in our life. In fact, one of the worst things you can do in times of sorrow is to sit and do nothing. If sorrow is dominating your life, seek out your divine duty and get busy doing it. It will help you as it did Samuel. Samuel needed to stop mourning and start moving. So do many of us today and doing our duty will help to end the mourning and energize the movement.

Samuel was not the only one who was mourning and in misery because of Saul when the anointing of David took place. Many in Israel were also in misery because of Saul's ruling of the nation. Saul was not much of an inspirer for people during his reign. Most of the time, he caused despair in the hearts of the people. 1 Samuel 13:6 records the people were distressed, and further records "*and all the people followed him trembling.*" Saul did not help matters either by letting the people disobey God's command and taking other forbidden spoils of the Amalekites. Like a poor ruler, Saul encouraged evil in the land. And evil brings misery, not happiness, to its followers. So evil rulers do not bring happiness to a land but cause mourning instead. "*When the righteous are in authority the people rejoice but when the wicked rule, the people mourn*" (Proverbs 29:2 KJV). The next time you do not think character is necessary in a ruler of a nation as some seem to think in our day, think on this verse in Proverbs and on the misery of Israel because of Saul's rule, and you will change your mind. Character is the foremost qualification for a good ruler of a nation.

"*If a ruler harkens to lies, all his servants are wicked*" (Proverbs 29:12 KJV).

Another dark condition in Israel at the time of David's anointing was the madness of Saul. After David was anointed by Samuel, the madness of Saul became much more evident because "*The spirit of the Lord departed from Saul and an evil spirit of the Lord troubled him.*" (1 Samuel 16:14 KJV). This resulted in erratic and threatening behavior by Saul, such as, throwing the javelin several times at David, hunting David's life incessantly, ordering the killing of a host of priests, and going to a witch for help. But this madness was already evidencing itself before David was anointed. This is especially seen in respect to his decree to have his own son Jonathan killed. Saul, who on one occasion mercifully forbid the slaying of those who opposed him (1 Samuel 11:12-13). Later demanded the death for his son Jonathan because Jonathan had broken Saul's order forbidding his army to eat when in a battle against the Philistines (1 Samuel 14:24). Jonathan did not hear the order, so when they found honey, he ate it and was strengthened to do battle (1 Samuel 14:27). Jonathan was the one who caused Israel to win a great battle over the Philistines at that time. Yet Saul, in his madness, wanted to kill Jonathan because Jonathan unknowingly broke Saul's rule and a very disabling order. Jonathan's fellow soldiers prevented Saul from killing Jonathan, but such bizarre orders and thinking of Saul showed the great madness and how poorly he was ruling his country. Anyone who disagreed with him, he came against them. His rule did not reflect wisdom or justice. All of this underscored the need for a new King, a need David will fill so well.

1 Samuel 16:1–3 (KJV): *And the Lord said unto Samuel, How long wilt thou mourn for Saul, seeing I have rejected him from reigning over Israel? fill thine horn with oil, and go, I will send thee to Jesse the Beth-lehemite: for I have provided me a king among his sons. And Samuel said, How can I go? if Saul hear it, he will kill me. And the Lord said, Take a heifer with thee, and say, I am come to sacrifice to the Lord. And call Jesse to the sacrifice, and I will shew thee what thou shalt do: and thou shalt anoint unto me him whom I name unto thee.*

The horn was either a manmade vessel shaped like a horn or else an actual Ram's horn. In either case, it was designated to administer the sanctified anointment oil, whose formula is described in Exodus 30:22-25.

The act of anointing a king had to be performed by a Prophet. The oil was poured on his head, smeared in the form of a Crown between his eyebrows, and the remainder again poured on his head. The amount of oil used was the amount that filled the horn (Radack).

Hannah alluded to this horn in her prophetic song first Samuel chapter two. This implied that only the king whom her son Samuel would anoint with the horn would enjoy an extensive reign, whereas the reign of those whose anointments were made with a flask, i.e., Saul and Jehu would not last long. Jehovah chose Saul in response to and as a way of satisfying the will of the people. In that case, he did not send the prophet to anoint the king as his emissary but had the prospective king go to the prophet. In this case, when Jehovah chose the candidate to represent his Kingdom without reference to the will of the people, he sent the prophet to the king. The two verbs in the phrase go and I shall send you seems contradictory. For a command, implies that the Prophet is to proceed on his own, whereas I shall send you connotes that he will be acting as God's Messenger. Thus, when Jehovah requests that something corrective be done, he tells the prophet to act as if he were acting independently. Accordingly, go implies that the Prophet shall of his own initiative bring misfortune upon the soul by devastating him of his Kingdom, which will have the effect of causing the spirit of Jehovah to depart from him first. The second phrase, I shall send you, does expressly state Jehovah's involvement, for it refers to the good fortune of David.

Jesse, his father, belongs to the tribe of Judah. His father, Obed, was the son of Boaz and Ruth.

The Benjamite means that Jesse resided in the Judean city of Bethlehem, where his grandfather Boaz had lived. Bethlehem was a very small place. It was so small it was not even mentioned in the list of cities of Judah in the book of Joshua 15:20-63; compare the description given of Bethlehem in Micah 5:2. Smallness is not a handicap to greatness. Bethlehem is a very significant location regardless of its size. It was where Rachel gave birth to Benjamin and died in the process. It was where Boaz married Ruth the great-grand-mother of David. And many centuries after David was anointed there, Jesus Christ was born there. You may be in Bethlehem in the eyes of the world, you may be small and unnoticed and not on anyone's map of importance, but that will not stop you from being used greatly in God's service. God is not concerned about your bigness in the eyes of man. He is chiefly concerned about how big your dedication is to him.

"For I have seen for myself a king among his sons" (1 Samuel 16:7 KJV).

I have seen implies that David's fitness for kingship was not readily apparent, and only Jehovah detected it.

Also, Jehovah initially left the identity of the specific son concealed for two reasons: first, to indicate that Jesse's entire household was spiritually distinguished, and second, to teach the type of flaws that disqualify a person from sitting on the throne, as we will see.

Samuel asked, *"How can I go if Saul finds out, he will kill me?"*

Presumably, Samuel was concerned that Saul would view his anointing another man king as an offense punishable by death. Alternatively, Samuel was not worried when questioning Jehovah's command. Rather, his question *"how can I go"* may be read as, *"in what manner shall I go?"* Earlier, Samuel's error in showing mercy to the Amalekites' animals had been derived from his understanding of the law of the decapitated heifer (1 Samuel 15:5). Samuel's evocation of the law would remind Saul to show mercy to Samuel. Let us not forget in verse 3 where Jehovah said, *"and called Jesse to the sacrifice, and I will show thee what thou shall do, and thou shalt anointed unto me him who I name unto thee."*

When those who were ordered to the sacrificial service had arrived, it is obvious that Samuel felt both a sense of confidence and relief. Surely before him would be Jehovah's next choice to be King. As the sons were ordered to proceed forward, He looked at Eliab and said, surely the Lord's anointed his before him, verse 6. When it came time for Samuel to choose one of Jesse's sons to be anointed as king, he was impressed. In the view of what verse 7 says, we can conclude that Eliab was impressive to look at from a physical standpoint because of the impressive appearance. Samuel said, *"Surely the Lord's anointing is before him."* Samuel thought for sure he was the choice for the new king because outwardly, he looked so kingly. But Samuel had used the wrong principle for choosing a King. Therefore, God quickly corrected Samuel's thinking by saying, *"Look not on his countenance, on the height of his stature, because I have refused him."* **THE LAST THING WE NEED IS ANOTHER SAUL!**

Samuel is not the only one who gets excited about the outward appearance. Men universally have this problem, and they have had the problem from the very beginning of their existence. It started in Eden. The outward appearance deceived Eve, for the fruit of the forbidden tree "was pleasant to the eyes" Genesis 3:6. Outward appearance has seduced multitudes in every age. There are scarcely any rules so deceptive as the rule of appearance. The Apostle Paul warned us against the attraction of appearance in the area of covetousness. In verse 7, Samuel is informed clearly that "The Lord looketh on the heart." The principle that must guide our choice is a good heart. Judging by the heart principle means that in making choices, the character of a person is more important than the countenance, faith is more important than the face, morals are more important than what you see in the mirror.

In Samuel's effort to find the right one for king, there were a lot of opportunities to compromise. Jesse had seven sons that Samuel looked over before he saw David. When the eldest son Eliab was refused by God, Samuel then went on to Abinadab, the next son of Jesse. He too was rejected by God. Samuel then examined the third son Shammah and on through the first seven sons of Jesse. When Samuel finished going through these, there seemed to be no other sons. If Samuel had been like many others, he would have disregarded God's instructions and compromised by selecting one of the seven. But Samuel did not do that. Rather, he asked Jesse, "*Are all your sons here?*" (1 Samuel 16:11).

The Midrash teaches that Hashem tests whether "*his righteous ones*" (Psalm 11:5) are fit to be leaders by making them shepherds! When David tended his sheep, he would first feed the youngest sheep tender grass, then feed the oldest sheep fresh grass, and finally feed the strongest sheep the toughest grass. Since he knew how to tend to each sheep's individual needs, Hashem appointed him to do the same for the people of Israel; thus (Psalm 78:70-71 KJV), "*He chose David, his servant, and took him from the sheep corrals. From behind the nursing ewes, He brought him to tend to Jacob his nation, and to Israel, his inheritance.*"

Samuel knew that it had to be at least one of the sons because Jehovah had told him that he would choose the candidate, and he had not yet given the indication of having done so. From these verses, it appears that Jesse had denied his son and thus neglected to send for him. Moreover, even after he acknowledged David's existence in response to Samuel's questioning him, he still proposed that they sit down to eat without first calling David. Jesse certainly knew that Samuel had come as a Prophet and emissary of Jehovah to anoint one of his sons as King. Why then did he act in this fashion?

A number of sources addressed this issue, and in the course of which they also deal with some puzzling comments that David makes about himself in Psalms. For example, David says, "B*ehold, in iniquity was I fashioned an in sin did my mother conceived me"* (Psalm 51:5 KJV). To what iniquity and sin is he referring? Also, David says, *"I became a stranger unto my brothren, and alien to my mother's children"* (Psalm 69:9 KJV). Why was that the case?

As we have seen, Ruth's marriage to Boaz was marred by controversy since she descended from Moab and the Torah prohibits Moabites from marrying into the Jewish nation (Deuteronomy 23:4). Boaz headed a court that ruled that this prohibition applied only to Moabite males, not females, and thus he permitted himself to marry Ruth. Yet doubts still remained, particularly when Boaz died the day after his marriage, which was interpreted as a sign of divine disapproval.

Thus, although Obed, Jesse, and his sons were respected Jews some question whether their Jewish status still lingered. Therefore, after having fathered six sons, Jesse began to suspect that he was a Moabite and forbidden to remain married to a Jewish woman, and he accordingly separated himself from her.

After a few years passed, he wanted to have more children and so devised the following plan. He had a non-Jewish maidservant, who he proposed to marry in the following manner. He would free her on condition that he was not a Moabite, so that she might become a full-fledged Jew, and he would then marry her. Should he be a Moabite, the act of manumission would be void. Then he would marry her as a gentile, their children would not have the status of Moabites, and they would be converted to Judaism.

Hearing this proposal, the maidservant felt sorry for Jesse's wife. She agreed to the proposal but apprised Jesse's wife of the plan; on the wedding night, the two women secretly exchanged places (as Rachel and Leah had done). Thus, that night Jesse unknowingly caused his first wife and not the maidservant to conceive.

When Jesse's wife grew visibly pregnant, apparently from an adulterous relationship, her sons thought she was liable for the death penalty. As for the child, who was David, he was considered to be illegitimate, and since he was viewed as an embarrassment to the family, he was sent into the wilderness as a shepherd, away from the public eye.

David's mother did not reveal the facts of the matter as not to embarrass Jesse, also not to reveal what the maid had done. As a result, David was estranged by his brothers. They did not consider him a brother, and Jesse did not consider him his son.

Until he was 28, David tended the sheep in the wilderness, and his father and brothers expected to hear that a lion or bear had slaughtered him. But instead of growing bitter, he spent those years attaching himself to Jehovah, singing his praises, accepting humiliation, and accepting Jehovah's will. Also, he associated with sages until he developed into an exceptional Torah scholar.

When Samuel arrived, therefore, Jesse saw no reason to summon David. Since he had not realized that David was his son, only after his other sons were not chosen did Jesse begin to wonder if Samuel was referring to David. Finally, when David came, and Samuel anointed him, Jesse understood what had happened. He realized that David was his child and was holy, pure, and fit to be king.

All seem to agree that immediately after his anointment, David was charged with divine inspiration that gave him wisdom, strength, confidence to kill a lion and bear, defeat Goliath, the ability to play and compose the psalms, and succeed in his every endeavor. The spirit was transferred from Saul to David to be **KING**. Saul is King, but David is now the anointed choice of Jehovah. As in the study of types, shadows, and patterns we see that Jehovah sometimes uses different manifestations for revelations and interpretations of his will for his people. Oftentimes lessons are learned in threes. We have constant reminders of Father, Son, Holy Spirit; good, acceptable, perfect; 30,60,100; faith, hope, charity; spirit, soul, body; Outer Court, Holy Place, and Holy of All; Abraham, Isaac, and Jacob; Peter, James, and John. There is nothing new under the sun, even the satan wants to steal, kill, and destroy.

This is the first anointing, there will be two more. After David was anointed by Samuel, a number of years passed before David actually became King; but those years were not idle or wasted years. During those years, many events transpired which helped to train and prepare David for the throne. David took an interesting position in his heart, while he was clear that Samuel had anointed him to be king, he was also clear that Saul was still in the chair. Such great wisdom for a young man with no political experience. David responded to this high call by going back to his sheep. The impressive level of grace on his life led him back to the wilderness. It is there when left alone with God, the actual tutorial begins. David learned that every great man must spend time in the wilderness. Abraham wondered looking for a city, Moses was driven, Jesus was led, Paul chose to go to Arabia, but the wilderness is a must that reveals His purpose, plan, and strength in you. It was the testimony of David to Goliath that he'd killed a bear and lion with only his hands by the aid of Jehovah. The Talmud teaches a Jew succeeds in war when he places his trust in Hashem, a trust that he fortifies when he recited the Shema (the Jewish confession of faith made up of three scriptural texts: Deuteronomy. 6:4-9, 11:13-21; Numbers 15:37-41). The mandated times for reciting the Shema are morning and evening. It was precisely at these times that Goliath came to challenge the Jews, in order to prevent them from doing so. According to the Talmud, this corresponds to the forty-day period during which God gave the Jewish people the Torah. Just as it took the Jews forty days to receive the Torah, so did it take them forty days to develop the spiritual fortitude to overcome Goliath (Radak). The Talmud states that in his arrogance, Goliath challenged Hashem Himself, "Who is this God," "Man of War" (Exodus 15:3). There's hardly a man alive that doesn't know how this story ended! With great grace on his life, and the total absence of fear, David presented his King with victory over the Philistines. Even though he had been anointed by Samuel, the time was not yet to move forward. His passion needed to be trained! Instead of hastening to replace Saul, David became a servant to the man he would replace. I suppose it was David who set the pattern that Elisha should serve Elijah. What a healthy, godly approach to Kingdom ministry, that even though the King has been limited in time, Jehovah has not chosen to empty the chair yet. He knows the anointment really births a season of training. Here is a lesson that so often young anointed ministers have fallen short of. Once the anointment happens, they lack the discipline to develop the call on their life. Too many times assumption has cancelled greatness. David is functioning under the blessing, while Saul is functioning under the curse. The direction of life could not be more different; however, David submits to being Saul's armor-bearer and also his chief musician even under the constant threat of death by javelin.

After the victory of David and the death of Goliath, it became more obvious that Saul begun spiraling at a faster pace.

David was King elect, yet another wore the Crown. Jesse's son had been anointed to the throne, yet Saul was now persecuting him. Had God forgotten to be gracious? Let us be minded that faith must be tested, to prove its genuineness. Yet only he who gives faith, can maintain it; and for this we must constantly seek him. Concerning Hezekiah, we are told *"God left him, to try him, that he might know all that was in his heart"* (2 Chronicles 32:31 KJV). Yet, being a man of like passions with our own, and the supernatural grace of God supporting him at the time. Instead of David's fears being thoroughly removed to trust God and waiting quietly with Samuel to receive a word of divine guidance, he was occupied with self-preservation and the immediate danger from Saul. This caused him to lie to Ahimelech the priest of Nob by means of which he obtained bread. But the fearful cost of the lie caused Saul to seek vengeance. Thus, he commanded Doeg in slaying 85 of those who wore the linen ephod. Disastrous indeed are the consequences when we seek to have our own way and path for ourselves. How differently had things turned out if David trusted the Lord and trusted him for protection.

Let us also be reminded that when a saint is out of touch with God, when he is in a backslidden state, his behavior is so different from his former conduct, so inconsistent with his profession, that his actions now present a strange enigma. There is no way of determining how far a backslider may go, or how foolishly and madly he may act. David was worried about being unarmed, an asked the high priest if there were weapons to be used. On being informed that the only one available was *"the sword of Goliath,"* which had been preserved in the Tabernacle as a memorial of the Lord's goodness to his people, David exclaimed *"There is none like it, give it to me"* (1 Samuel 21:9). Motivated by fear, David now takes refuge in Gaff of the Philistines. There appears to be an ungodly pattern with the backslidden Christian, that he will fraternize with the world. He attempts to conceal his colors, hoping that he will not be recognized as a follower of the Lord Jesus. *"And the servants of Achish said unto him, is not this David the King of the land*?" (1 Samuel 21:11 KJV). They did not sing one to another of him and dance, saying Saul had slain his thousands and David his ten thousands. God will not allow his people to remain undetected. David was quickly recognized. David soon learned from the shame of his folly that he had not walked in wisdom. Not only was David deeply humiliated by this episode, but Jehovah was grievously dishonored thereby.

"David therefore departed thence and escaped to The Cave Adullam." The underground asylum of David made an admirable closet for prayer. It's very solitude being helpful for the exercise of devotion. C.H. Spurgeon said, *"Had David prayed as much in his Palace as he did in his cave, he might never have fallen into the act which brought such misery upon his latter day."* How often have we passed through these painful experiences and bitter disappointments before we thoroughly learn this lesson? Here we behold the son of Jesse turning to the only one who could help. This is what we should do, thoroughly casting our care on him who loves us. This was the hour of David's unpopularity, he was outlawed from the court, a fugitive from Saul, and he was dwelling in a cave. Now was the time for devotion to be clearly exhibited. But only those who truly loved him could be expected to support him while danger and persecution was still present. *"And when his brethren and all his father's house heard it, they went down thither to him"* (1 Samuel 22:1 KJV). True love is unaffected by the outward circumstances of its object. When the heart is genuinely knit to another, a change in his fortunes will not produce a change in its affections. David might be, in the eyes of the world, in disgrace, but that made no difference to those who loved him. He might be living in a cave, but that was all the more reason why they should show their kindness and

demonstrate under unquestionable loyalty. Among other things, this painful trial enabled David to discover who were, and who were not his real friends.

Even in your darkest days, God will prove his choices in leadership. *"And everyone that was in distress, and everyone that was in debt, and everyone that was discontented, gathered themselves unto him"* (1 Samuel 22:2 KJV). What a strange company to seek for God's anointed. There is no mention made of the captains of the army, the men of state, the Prince is of the region, coming unto David. No, they, with all like them, preferred the court and the Palace to the Cave of Adullam. What a handful compared with the hosts of Israel! But did Christ fare any better in the days of his flesh? How many friends stood around the cross, wept at his sepulcher, or greeted him as he burst the bars of death? How many followed him to Bethany, gazed at his ascending form, or gathered in the upper room to await the promised Spirit? Your wilderness experience may be a lonely, dry, and upsetting place but rest assured that the victory is promised, and your enemies will fall! We should note that Saul and all who would be a successor to his throne from his house suffered tragic ends in a battle with the Philistines in the Valley of Jezreel. Saul would not be captured and chose to fall on his own sword.

David mourned the death of Saul. There is an unspoken respect that's seldom mentioned in the tumultuous relationship between Saul and David. Very few choose to tackle the timing of David's life when you hear him referred to Saul as "my father." "*Moreover, my father, see, Ye, see the skirt of thy robe in my hand: for in that I cut off the skirt of thy robe, and kill thee not, know thou and see that there is neither evil nor transgression in my hand, and I have not sinned against thee; Yet thou huntest my soul to take it*" (1 Samuel 24:11 KJV). According to Targum, my father is a term of respect indicating my master. The Midrash on the other hand, states that David was addressing Saul as his father since Saul was his father-in-law. From this infers that "a person is as obligated to honor his father-in-law as his father." Even though the attacks on David's life were very real, there's something about God's anointing that automatically breeds respect and teaches grace even in the midst of a storm. This is not the only surprise in this relationship. When David rebuked Abner, Saul's general, for not keeping close watch over the king and his spear, while his water near his head had been removed, Saul recognized David's voice and said, "*Is that your voice, my son David?*" David replied, "*It is my voice, my Lord, the King.*" And he said, "*Why does my Lord pursue his servant for what have I done and what evil is in my hand?*" (1 Samuel 26:17-18 KJV). Abner had not recognized David's voice. But Saul, who had spent much time with David did. Saul refers to David as his son since David had twice shown him mercy. Saul's question was not intended to ascertain David's identity.

Rather, he asked if David's tone of voice and words, which indicated that he viewed Saul as a father, were sincere. One interpretation given asks *"Are those sincere words of my son David?"* (Kli Yakar).

The fugitive years of David were now over, and the long wait from his private anointing by Samuel to the ascending of the throne of Israel was also over. Much had happened in David's life since that day a dozen or more years earlier when he was summoned from his lowly shepherd duties to be privately anointed by the Prophet Samuel as Israel's next King. Since that day, David had gone through a number of very painful experiences which prepared him well for the duties of the King of Israel. Whenever God calls us to be honorable, privileged, and important posts of duty, you can be sure that he will give us much training for the task. The training may take years and be very rough at times, but God does not put one into a position of great responsibility without ample preparation. Sometimes when we become aware that we are chosen for an important task, our egos become inflated. But that inflated ego, which will hinder our performance and is ignorant of our inabilities, will be deflated in God's rigorous school of preparation, a school which replaces inability with ability, foolishness with wisdom, immaturity with maturity, and carnality with spirituality.

We have noted that Saul is dead, and now destiny has put its hand in the heart of the future king, but David has learned that timing and His will are absolutes when it involves the will of God. *"David inquired of the Lord, saying, shall I go up into any of the cities of Judah?"* (2 Samuel 2:1 KJV). In David's request to God about moving forward, we note the wisdom of seeking the will of God, and the waiting in seeking the will of God. To the natural eye Ziglag did not seem like the place where David should reign as King over Israel. But David would not run ahead of God by leaving Ziglag without God's orders. He would not move until God said to move, and in his situation, this was really commendable for David. For at that time, Ziglag was a desolate city. It had just been burned to the ground. But *"though Ziglag be in ruins, he would not quit without direction from God"* (Henry). He will wait for divine orders before moving. David's attitude here is not easy to practice when the place where you are now staying is very undesirable. Sometimes, when we are in a comfortable location, we do not want to leave to do God's will. It's easy to remain despondent and depressed. David's location however, was the opposite. It was a place where you would be anxious to leave. But he waited for God's orders before leaving even though he was in a desolate place.

If your place in life is currently a desolate place, be careful that you do not look only at the circumstances before you move. Make sure you have God's orders before moving. Pastors who are in church situations like that of Ziglag need encouragement and exhortation. Please take caution and not be anxious to jump to another pastorate without divine orders. It might work is not the answer that will bring his presence. It may be hard to stay at a Ziglag church, but moving before you have God's orders will prove to be a lot worse, even if the new place you moved to has an abundance of exciting amenities. Let's also pause to remember that even though Ziglag was an undesirable location, Jehovah had given David favor and reward while he was there. 1 Chronicles chapter 12 gives us detailed information that the book of Samuel does not. While many great men joined David a very impressive scripture rings out to me in 1 Chronicles, chapter 12 verse 21 (KJV), *"And they helped David against the band of the Rovers: for they were all mighty men of valor and were captains in the host. For at that time day by day there came to David to help him,* **until it was a great host, like the host of God."**

David had already been privately anointed by Samuel some dozen or so years earlier. But now comes the first of two public anointings for David. A private anointing before a public anointing is not unique; Saul was also privately anointed in 1 Samuel 10 before he was publicly anointed 1 Samuel 11: 14-15.

2 Samuel 2: 1 (KJV), *"And it came to pass after this, that David inquired of the Lord saying, shall I go up into any of the cities of Judah? And the Lord said to him, go up. And David said, whither shall I go up? And he said, until Hebron. So, David went up thither, and his two wives also, Ahinoam the*

Jezreelitess, and Abigail Nabal's wife the Carmelite. And his men that were with him did David bring up, every man with his household: and they dwelt in the cities of Hebron. And the men of Judah came, and there they anointed David King over the House of Judah. And the men of Judah, came and there they anointed David King over the House of Judah."

Though David was now a King, His troubles did not cease. It is true that many of his troubles ended when he became King. But he soon had a new set of troubles. These troubles were not as perilous to him as Saul's murderous actions were, but some of them were still very serious in nature. These aggravations, like his previous troubles, opposed his work for God. The enemy will always oppose God's work. If he cannot stop David from being a King, then he will try to hinder David as king. 2 Samuel 3:1 (KJV), *"Now there was long war between the House of Saul in the House of David: but David waxed stronger and stronger, and the House of Saul waxed weaker and weaker."* The aggravation between the dynasty of Saul and David's Kingdom caused civil war. Although it was a trying struggle, it was a triumphant struggle. The struggle between the House of Saul and the House of David is described as a *"long war."* It was an extended struggle, for over seven years. The length of the struggle did not indicate the weakness of right but the persistence of wrong. Wrong does not give up easily. So again, and again we must battle against it if we are to win. A note of caution; don't despair over the length of the struggle; though trying as it may be, it brings much opportunity for the growth of our patience and faith. (Romans 5:3) *"tribulation works patience."* The enemy really means business. It's not playing games. It wants to destroy God's work. Evil will be the aggressor. It will violate the laws of life and shed blood unjustly. God's program will always be opposed, and it will be opposed strongly. Let us be as earnest for the Kingdom of light as evil people are for the kingdom of the darkness. Time is in favor of the righteous!

There is a vast difference between the promises of God and his eternal decrees: many of the former are conditional, whereas the latter are immutable, dependent upon nothing for their fulfillment save the omnipotence of God. In saying that, many of the divine promises recorded in Holy Writ are conditional. We do not mean they are uncertain and unreliable; we mean that they are infallible declarations of what God will do or give providing we follow a *certain* course of conduct, just as the divine threatening recorded in scripture are a declaration of what God will do or inflict if a different course be pursued. God has declared (1 Samuel 2:30 KJV), *"Wherefore the Lord God of Israel saith, I said indeed that thy house, and the house of thy father, should walk before me for ever: but now the Lord saith, Be it far from me; for them that honour me I will honour, and they that despise me shall be lightly esteemed."* On the other hand, it is equally a fact that those who would not be subject to God's word, who follow instead the devices of their own hearts and give way to the lusts of the flesh, suffer adversity and come under the rod of divine chastisement; of them, it has to be said, "*your sins have withholden good things from you*" (Jeremiah 5:25). They have missed God's best: not that they have failed to obtain any blessings which he had eternally decreed should be theirs, but they have not entered into the good of what God's word promises should be the present portion of those who walk in obedience.

Likewise, the book of Deuteronomy chapter 28 has similar stipulations; "A*nd it shall come to pass, **if** thou shall hearken diligently unto the voice of the Lord that God, to **observe** and to **do** all his commandments which I command thee this day, that the Lord thy God will set thee on high above all nations of the earth: and all these blessings shall come on thee and overtake thee, **if** thou shall hearken unto the voice of the Lord thy God*" (Deuteronomy 28:1 KJV). It is here where we come to another transitional and pivotal point in David's life.

"*Then came all the tribes of Israel to David unto Hebron, and spake, saying, Behold, we are thy bone and thy flesh. Also in time past, when Saul was king over us, thou wast he that leddest out and broughtest in Israel: and the Lord said to thee, Thou shalt feed my people Israel, and thou shalt be a captain over Israel. So all the elders of Israel came to the king to Hebron; and king David made a league with them in Hebron before the Lord: and they anointed David king over Israel.*

David was thirty years old when he began to reign, and he reigned forty years. In Hebron he reigned over Judah seven years and six months: and in Jerusalem he reigned thirty and three years over all Israel and Judah" (2 Samuel 5:1-5 KJV).

With Ish-Bosheth, Saul's son, now dead, the way was clear for David to assert his sovereignty over the Northern tribes of Israel as well as over Judah. There was a general recognition in the North that this should be done, so a delegation from all the tribes went to Hebron to encourage David's rule over them. They pointed out that they were his kinsmen, his own flesh and blood, that is, all were descendants of Jacob. They stated that he had distinguished himself as a hero of Israel. But furthermore, they were conscious of the calling and anointing of the Lord in bringing David to power to shepherd them.

With no further hesitation they installed him as king over the entire nation. David reciprocated by entering into covenant with them. Samuel's earlier oil-anointing of David (1 Samuel 16:13) demonstrated God's choice of David. This third oil-anointing, like his second anointing in Hebron over Judah (2 Samuel 2:4), was the people's confirmation of that choice and a public installation. It is worth noting Moses saw this day and left instructions for His people. David's covenant probably involved an oath in which he pledged to follow the Mosaic requirements for kingship (Deuteronomy 17:14–20 KJV). *When thou art come unto the land which the Lord thy God giveth thee, and shalt possess it, and shalt dwell therein, and shalt say, I will set a king over me, like as all the nations that are about me; Thou shalt in any wise set him king over thee, whom the Lord thy God shall choose: one from among thy brethren shalt thou set king over thee: thou mayest not set a stranger over thee, which is not thy brother. But he shall not multiply horses to himself, nor cause the people to return to Egypt, to the end that he should multiply horses: forasmuch as the Lord hath said unto you, Ye shall henceforth return no more that way. Neither shall he multiply wives to himself, that his heart turn not away: neither shall he greatly multiply to himself silver and gold. And it shall be, when he sitteth upon the throne of his kingdom, that he shall write him a copy of this law in a book out of that which is before the priests the Levites: And it shall be with him, and he shall read therein all the days of his life: that he may learn to fear the Lord his God, to keep all the words of this law and these statutes, to do them: That his heart be not lifted up above his brethren, and that he turn not aside from the commandment, to the right hand, or to the left: to the end that he may prolong his days in his kingdom, he, and his children, in the midst of Israel.*

(2 Samuel 5:4–5) David began his reign at age 30, the age at which priests began to serve (Numbers 4:3; 1 Chronicles 23:3). After seven and one-half years at Hebron, David decided to relocate the capital. His reason was almost certainly political for he decided on Jerusalem, a city on the

border between Judah and the Northern tribes. The distinction between Israel and Judah (2 Samuel 11:11; 12:8; 19:42–43; 24:1, 9) indicates that 2 Samuel was written after the nation was divided in 931 B.C. into the Northern and Southern Kingdoms.

(2 Samuel 5:6–9) Since Jerusalem had remained in Jebusite control ever since the days of Joshua (Joshua 15:63) it was considered neutral, so David's residence there would demonstrate tribal impartiality. But the very fact that Jerusalem had remained in Jebusite control indicated its security and defensibility. This is seen clearly in the taunting response of its citizens to David's siege of the city. *Even the blind and the lame can ward you off,* they said.

Taking up a position on Mount Zion, the City of David, which lay just south of the Jebusite city, David promised his men that whoever could discover a means of access to the city would be promoted to commander-in-chief (1 Chronicles 11:6). The account in 1 Chronicles relates that Joab was able to do so, apparently by passing through the water tunnel which connected Jerusalem's water supply to its interior reservoirs (2 Samuel 5:8). The city was entered and incorporated into the capital.

So insulting to David was the Jebusite sarcasm about "the blind and lame," that it became proverbial to speak of his enemies in general as the blind and lame. After the city was captured, Mount Zion and Mount Ophel were consolidated into one entity described here and elsewhere as the City of David (2 Samuel 5:7, 9; 6:12; 1 Kings 2:10).

(2 Samuel 5:10–12) David's capture, expansion, and occupation of Jerusalem made it clear to all Israel and to surrounding peoples as well that God ... was with him and that he was not a renegade tribal chieftain but a political power with whom they must reckon. This is seen in the attention he received from Hiram, king of the Phoenician city-state of Tyre, who provided materials and men to build David a palace (1 Kings 5:1–11 KJV). *And Hiram king of Tyre sent his servants unto Solomon; for he had heard that they had anointed him king in the room of his father: for Hiram was ever a lover of David. And Solomon sent to Hiram, saying, Thou knowest how that David my father could not build an house unto the name of the Lord his God for the wars which were about him on every side, until the Lord put them under the soles of his feet. But now the Lord my God hath given me rest on every side, so that there is neither adversary nor evil occurrent. And, behold, I purpose to build an house unto the name of the Lord my God, as the Lord spake unto David my father, saying, Thy son, whom I will set upon thy throne in thy room, he shall build an house unto my name. Now therefore command thou that they hew me cedar trees out of Lebanon; and my servants shall be with thy servants: and unto thee will I give hire for thy servants according to all that thou shalt appoint: for thou knowest that there is not among us any that can skill to hew*

timber like unto the Sidonians. And it came to pass, when Hiram heard the words of Solomon, that he rejoiced greatly, and said, Blessed be the Lord this day, which hath given unto David a wise son over this great people. And Hiram sent to Solomon, saying, I have considered the things which thou sentest to me for: and I will do all thy desire concerning timber of cedar, and concerning timber of fir. My servants shall bring them down from Lebanon unto the sea: and I will convey them by sea in floats unto the place that thou shalt appoint me, and will cause them to be discharged there, and thou shalt receive them: and thou shalt accomplish my desire, in giving food for my household. So Hiram gave Solomon cedar trees and fir trees according to all his desire. And Solomon gave Hiram twenty thousand measures of wheat for food to his household, and twenty measures of pure oil: thus gave Solomon to Hiram year by year.

To all those who feel forgotten, just know that God knows how to send a Hiram into your life!

Recognition by a person of such stature convinced David that God indeed had established him and exalted his kingdom.

Chapter Three
The Ark Has Turned Aside!

S hortly after becoming King over all Israel, David attempted to recover the "Ark of God" for Jerusalem. This would be the most significant work for David. The great significance of the work comes from the great importance of the Ark. The Ark was the most important piece of furniture in the Tabernacle, which Moses had constructed in the wilderness. It was a wooden box covered in gold whose dimensions were approximately 2 feet in width by 4 feet in height by 10 feet in length. The cover on the box was called "the mercy seat." On its top covering there were two solid gold cherubim figures facing each other and covering the mercy seat with their wings. Inside the Ark were three items, Hebrews 9:4, the two tablets of stone, a pot of manna, and Aaron's rod that budded. The Ark was placed in the holy of holies, the most sacred part of the Tabernacle. Once a year. the high priest went into the holy of holies and sprinkled the atonement blood upon the mercy seat. That which made the ark the most important piece of furniture in the tabernacle was that it represented the presence of God: for God had said regarding the ark, "*There I will meet with thee, and I will commune with thee from above the mercy seat, and from between the two* Cherubims" (Exodus 25:22 KJV).

In typology the ark is also very significant in that it spoke of Jesus Christ. It spoke of Christ in at least three ways. The tablets of stone with the law written with the finger of God then spoke of Christ's obedience. He said, *"Yay, thy law is written within my heart" (*Psalm 40:8). The manna spoke of Christ the bread of life John 6:32-35. Aaron's rod that budded, Numbers 17 spoke of the resurrection of Christ. As we have already noted, it was the place where God communed with Israel. Christ is the one through whom we now commune with God. Jesus said, *"No man cometh unto the father, but by me"* (John 14:6). The consecration of the Ark with the atonement blood spoke of Christ. It is Christ's blood which provides mercy for the redemption of the sinner just as the blood upon the mercy seat provided atonement for Israel. Not just redemption, but in 1 John 2:2 we also find additional benefits, *"And he is the propitiation for our sins: and not for ours only, but also for the sins of the whole world."*

I am certain that David loved and cherished on the level that he could, the mighty and awesome relationship that he had with Jehovah. Even today, as we receive additional images of the invisible one who loves us, it gives you pause in believing that newly anointed King David totally understood the magnitude of his choice to restore the ark. In all that he did, it was still only a type of things to come. The word "TYPE" means "a foreshadowing:" that which takes place in a natural realm pointing to the "ANTITYPE" (substance or reality) of the "spiritual realm." Compare the Greek word "TUPOS." Favors Greek Lexicon adds that "TUPOS" is used in a doctrinal sense of a person or thing prefiguring a future messianic person or a thing. We studied the types of the Bible because our Lord spoke much of them (Luke 24:25-27 KJV). *Then he said unto them, O fools, and slow of heart to believe all that the prophets have spoken: Ought not Christ to have suffered these things, and to enter into his glory? And beginning at Moses and all the prophets, he expounded unto them in all the scriptures the things concerning himself."*

Romans 1:20 (KJV): *"For the invisible things of him from the creation of the world are clearly seen, being understood by the things that are made, even his eternal power and Godhead; so that they are without excuse."*

Colossians 2:17 (KJV): *"Which are a shadow of things to come; but the body is of Christ."*

Hebrews 8:5 (KJV): *"Who serve unto the example and shadow of heavenly things, as Moses was admonished of God when he was about to make the tabernacle: for, See, saith he, that thou make all things according to the pattern shewed to thee in the mount."*

Compare Abraham offered up his beloved son Isaac, Genesis 22 with John 3:16

The Passover lamb Exodus 12:1-23 with Matthew 26: 26-28; 1 Corinthians 5:7

The manna from heaven Exodus 16 with John 6:48-50; 1 Corinthians 10:16-17

The smitten rock Exodus 17 with 1 Corinthians 10:1-4

The nation of Israel the Old Testament Church, Acts 7:38; with 1 Corinthians 10:1-11

It's not difficult to think the Tabernacle is the old testament expression of JESUS! His house of flesh contained all the GLORY of the Father, all the fullness of the Godhead bodily (Colossians 1:19; 2:9). If you turn the structure on end, Brazen Altar (brass feet) Revelation 1, Water Laver in the middle (John 4), Candlestick and Table of Shewbread, outstretched hands, Golden Altar (heart), and Ark of the Covenant (HEAD) (Ephesians 1:22-23).

The Ark led Moses and the children of Israel through the wilderness and was used by Joshua when he came to the Jordan river and allowed everyone to arrive safely on the other side into Canaan. Shortly afterward, the Ark was carried around Jericho by the priest those 13 times before the walls of Jericho fell down. Later, in the degenerate days of Eli (when Samuel was his assistant), it passed into unholy use by being taken out into battle against the Philistines, unadvisedly.

The Philistines were the principal enemy of Israel during the period of the last of the Judges (Judges 10:6-8; 13-16). They were a non-Semitic people, whose origin was most likely in some other part of the Aegean Sea area. They came to Canaan in two different migrations, one as early as Abraham's time (2000 BC), and the other about (1200 BC). They lived in five main towns on the southern Canaan coast, Gaza, Ashkelon, Ekron, Gath, and Ashdod. They were technologically advanced, pioneering in the use of iron and other skills (1 Samuel 13:19-20). The primary God of their Patheon was Dagon; a deity also worshipped as a grain God. Some scholars suggest that the Philistine Dagon represented as having a human torso and upper body and a fishes' tail. It may well be that the originally seafaring Philistines brought their fish God with them to Canaan and then adapted him to the Semitic God Dagon because of their need to become a grain producing people (Judges 15:3:5).

When Israel was attacked by the Philistines at Aphek, about 25 miles West of Shiloh, the Israelites sent men to Shiloh to bring the Ark of the covenant to the battlefield, supposing that its presence, would turn the battle. The ark did represent the presence of the Lord in battle but only when the people carried it in faith and by divine leading. The Philistines were terrified when they knew the ark was in the camp of Israel, for they had heard about its association with Israel's mighty God who had brought the people out of Egypt more than 300 years before. However, they summonsed their courage, they fought on and defeated Israel. In the process, the ark was captured, and the sons of Eli, its keepers, were killed. When Eli learned that the ark had been taken by the Pagan Philistines and that his sons were dead, he fell backward off his seat, broke his neck, and died. Shortly afterwards, his daughter-in-law, Phinehas' wife, died as she gave birth to a son whom she named appropriately enough, Ichabod, "there is no glory." Since the presence of the ark represented the presence of God in Israel, its capture suggested that not only was the ark gone, but God himself and all his glory was now in enemy hands.

The Philistines took the ark like a trophy of conquest to the temple of Dagon at Ashdod, about 50 miles Southwest. There they laid it at Dagon's feet as the victor, and the Lord was his prisoner. The next morning, Dagon lay prostrated before the ark. After they placed him back on his pedestal once again, Dagon, on the following day again, lay in submission before the Lord, this time shattered and broken, only his torso remained intact. His head and hands were broken off. Maybe someone should have given the Philistines a notice: "*Then he answered and spake unto me, saying, This is the word of the Lord unto Zerubbabel, saying, not by might, nor by power, but by my spirit, Saith the Lord of hosts*" (Zechariah 4:6 KJV).

The Philistine people fell under judgment as well, for the Lord sent a plague on the inhabitants of Ashdod; "*And it was so, that, after they had carried it about, the hand of the Lord was against the city with a very great destruction: and he smote the men of the city, both small and great, and they had emerods in their secret parts"(1 Samuel 5:9 KJV),* which evidently were carried by mice and cause large tumors to erupt in their body. After suffering the humiliation of their God and a plague, the Philistines decided to return the ark of the Lord to Israel. This may seem naive to modern readers, but the Philistines learned that God cannot be manipulated to their own convenience. They were advised by their own priests to send the ark back accompanied with tokens of tributes in the form of five gold tumors and five gold rats representing the five Philistine cities. These offerings to Israel's God would indicate their acknowledgment of his superiority (v5). Furthermore, the ark should be sent on a new driverless cart as a further test of the source of their troubles. If the two cows still nursing their young and not previously yoked (v7) pulled the cart directly back to Israel, it would be clear that Israel's God had indeed caused their affliction. But if they wandered aimlessly about, the Philistines could attribute their misfortune simply to chance.

The Israelites were so overjoyed to see the ark after seven months that they offered a sacrifice to the Lord at Beth Shemesh, the border town where the ark had been directed, about 15 miles west of Jerusalem. Unfortunately, the people of Beth Shemesh not only rejoiced at the return of the ark and offered sacrifices in worship, but they desecrated it by opening it and looking inside *"And he smote the men of Beth-*

shemesh, because they had looked into the ark of the Lord, even he smote of the people fifty thousand and threescore and ten men: and the people lamented, because the Lord had smitten many of the people with a great slaughter. And the men of Beth-shemesh said, Who is able to stand before this holy Lord God? and to whom shall he go up from us? And they sent messengers to the inhabitants of Kirjath-jearim, saying, The Philistines have brought again the ark of the Lord; come ye down, and fetch it up to you" (1 Sam 6:19-21 KJV). This violated the mosaic statute that only Levites could handle the Ark and not even they could touch it directly, or look there in (Numbers 4:5,15,20). Disobedience in this respect would bring death. The sin of the people of Beth Shemesh was a deliberate, intentional violation of the clear word of God. Scriptures record 50,070 were lost for that one particular act. The point, of course, is that not only unbelievers (the Philistines) suffer when the law of the Lord is disregarded, but believers (the Israelites) also suffer when they do not conform to his requirements. After this disaster, the ark was moved again (1 Samuel 6:21). This time to Kirjath- jearim. The ark remained in the custody of the family of Abinadab (1 Samuel 7:1) for about 100 years.

Again, David gathered together all the chosen men of Israel, thirty thousand. And David arose, and went with all the people that were with him from Baale of Judah, to bring up from thence the ark of God, whose name is called by the name of the Lord of hosts that dwelleth between the cherubims. And they set the ark of God upon a new cart, and brought it out of the house of Abinadab that was in Gibeah: and Uzzah and Ahio, the sons of Abinadab, drave the new cart. And they brought it out of the house of Abinadab which was at Gibeah, accompanying the ark of God: and Ahio went before the ark. And David and all the house of Israel played before the Lord on all manner of instruments made of fir wood, even on harps, and on psalteries, and on timbrels, and on cornets, and on cymbals. And when they came to Nachon's threshingfloor, Uzzah put forth his hand to the ark of God, and took hold of it; for the oxen shook it. And the anger of the Lord was kindled against Uzzah; and God smote him there for his error; and there he died by the ark of God. And David was displeased, because the Lord had made a breach upon Uzzah: and he called the name of the place Perez-uzzah to this day. And David was afraid of the Lord that day, and said, How shall the ark of the Lord come to me? So David would not remove the ark of the Lord unto him into the city of David: but David carried it aside into the house of Obed-edom the Gittite. And the ark of the Lord continued in the house of Obed-edom the Gittite three months: and the Lord blessed Obed-edom, and all his household (2 Sam. 6:1-11 KJV).

The first verse of 2 Samuel 6 recorded an incident that needs to be prayerfully laid to the heart of everyone that God has separated unto his service. It chronicles the most blessed action on the part of David, who had only the thought to bring honor and glory to the Lord. However, that action was sadly marred by permitting the fervency of his zeal to ignore the precepts of God. He was anxious that the neglected and dishonored Ark should be suitably housed in Zion. His desire was good, and his motive was pure, but his execution of the same met with the open displeasure of the Lord. It is not sufficient to have a worthy purpose and goodwill: God's work must be performed in the right way, that is, according to the rules of his prescribing; anything other than that is but a manifestation of self-will.

There seems to be many in Christendom today who desire to do a good work, but they are exceedingly lax and careless in the mode and manner in which their desires are carried out. They act as though the means used and the methods employed are of no importance, so long as their outcome is right. They are creatures of impulse while imitating the example of others. They seem to have no concern for God's standards, a lack of information as regards to studying his word, no interest to diligently discover what laws and rules the Lord has given for the regulation of our conduct in his "service." Consequently, they are governed by the flesh rather than the spirit, so that it frequently happens that they do good things in a wrong way, in a manner directly opposed to God's way as revealed in His word.

It appears as if in the life of some leaders, there is an absence to challenge their own actions against divine standards. There is no effort to inquire how close their activities are to His will or to measure up to the methods of God. All is well just as long as they appear to succeed; nothing else matters. However, inescapably the day of Isaiah 1:12 is coming: "*When ye come to appear before me, who hath required this at your hand, to tread my courts?*"

David's actions now prove that favor on your life is not enough! None of David's devices match the scriptures warranted to carry out this task. "*For I bear them record that they have a zeal of God, but not according to knowledge*" *(Romans 10:2 ESV). Also consider "Desire without knowledge is not good, and whoever makes haste with his feet misses his way" (Proverbs 19:2 ESV).*

So much is wrong with this picture; however, let us begin with Eleazar, son of Abinadab. As the priest consecrated to guard the Ark of the covenant while it remained in the House of his father, he should have known the way prescribed by God to Moses to move the holy ark. After almost 100 years, are we to believe he hadn't heard not to touch or handle with his hands the holy things?" Or maybe he had become so familiar with the ark that he became common with the anointing, no longer treasured the presence of God! Perhaps, with the remnants of Moses Tabernacle sitting on Mount Gibeon, there was a level of confusion to the sons of

Abinadab. Not only was Eleazar uninformed or misinformed, but so was Ahio and Uzzah. It is difficult to imagine all of the items of Moses Tabernacle present on Mount Gibeon, the brazen altar, the water labor, the Golden candlesticks, the table of bread, the Golden sensor; all being present and there is not one question "Where is the glory of God!"

Was ministry going on every day, day by day without the presence or the glory of God? Did we have a mountain full of priests without anyone missing the presence of Jehovah? Did leadership honestly allow work to go on in the name of protection without the protector? Was there ever a level of satisfaction without divine approval that a satisfactory work has been performed? Is it possible to become comfortable only with a title, to do a few duties, and no glory present? And did these sons who planned to move the Ark have mixed emotions about David's desire to take the Ark of God to Mount Zion and not to Mount Gibeon? That would mean two locations of worship, an old order, and a new order? Does this open the door for two visions? Is David really certain about where he wants this to go because our old King never required us to change?

The procession began with over 30,000 men of Israel. By any organizational standard, that's a pretty big church service! 1 Chronicles gives us a better look at the celebration, with all the instruments of music and the people's excitement as they disobediently handled the ark of God. Celebration should not be misinterpreted as approval! There was a lot of noise and dancing with no glory. Next, we note they took their directional cue from sinners. A new cart was brought for the ark (instead of a holy priest) the way the Philistines did after their curse. Instead of the sons of the prophet placing the glory on their shoulder (Numbers 4:15) (Luke 9:58), one chose to drive the cart while the other watched the atrocity forgetting the disobedient sons of Phineas. The wagon shook, the ark tilted, and Uzza tried to steady the ark of God where it was clear God didn't want to be. Uzza was killed because of his disobedience! It is here that the bible gives us a pivotal point in history: **"and David was afraid of the Lord that day"** verse 9. Heretofore, David only knew His love and kindness and never His wrath! However, because of this obvious offence and horrible act of disobedience, lessons must be learned. David has still some undeveloped areas in his life. *"The fear of the Lord is the beginning of wisdom: and the knowledge of the holy is understanding"* (Provers 9:10).

This location didn't happen by accident. It was at Nacon's threshing floor. The threshing floor was a common enough place. This is where the farmer would use the natural wind to help separate the grain from what's called "chaff." The word "chaff" means "rubbish." So, this was just the other parts of the grain that wouldn't be used. The farmer would use what is called a "winnowing fork" to throw up the chaff and the grain that was mixed together. This was just a shovel that looked like a fork. The wind would blow away the chaff and the heavy grains would fall back onto the threshing floor. The process was then repeated until only the grain was left. The grain could then be picked up and used to make bread. This process was so ordinary during biblical times that many didn't even think twice about it. *"And he shall be like a tree planted by the rivers of water, that bringeth forth his fruit in his season; His leaf also shall not wither; And whatsoever he doeth shall prosper. The ungodly are not so: But are like the chaff which the wind driveth away"* (Psalm 1:3,4).

While Ruth is in search of her kindred redeemer, she is told where to find him: *"And now is not Boaz of our kindred, with whose maidens thou wast? Behold, he winnoweth barley tonight in the threshingfloor"* (Ruth 3:2). God's purpose has always been His people be set apart. David was clearly following an example, not of God. God didn't need David to include the way of unsanctified sinners as a method to advance the kingdom. The way of the Philistines was desperately wrong, or perhaps he needed to silence the voice of those who followed the former king's neglect and stop a celebration that was in total error.

It's not that large of a stretch for me to take a look around and see so many similarities between my country and the Christian community. Paul talked about a form of Godliness but no power. Parades of crowds and music without examination for truth and power. Those who would give advice to the king, only for position and neglect to speak truth to power.

I can recall driving home from work, and a tent was put up. The sign said, "Miracles Nightly." I knew nothing about this new way of life and drove past for about a week. I finally got enough courage to go by and park a distance away. As I eased towards the tent, I heard, "In Jesus' name, be healed." My feet were glued to the grass as the person got up out of the wheelchair and walked, then began to run. I had never seen anything like this, but my heart felt at home and close to Him. I was so happy for the man as if I knew him, a wave of love came over me, and I wanted what I didn't understand. I asked, "Who is this man?" and the lady next to me said his name was R. W. Schambach. I wanted to shake his hand, but I feared that the anointing on his life would reveal who I was or wasn't. I became fascinated by the manifested presence of a loving God. I remember thinking, 'miracles are real.'

In my earlier days of salvation, I can vividly remember my pastor inviting us to pray with him. I was excited about the opportunity until he made it known it would be what was called "all night" prayer meeting. Being a new convert, I'm sure you can imagine I was taken back. Why would it take all night to tell God a few things? Certainly, all of us together could take a turn and still be out by 2. Here was a man who 'laid hands on me' and broke the bond of ten years of drugs off my life. I remember in a time of worship, I felt a great unexplained presence that I knew was the Lord and then Deacon Gladen, who had lost his sight began to bellow out from the front row "I CAN SEE, I CAN SEE." I watched him when Mother Car passed out in service and the nurses ran to her aid, only to look up with tears and said, "She's gone." My pastor never paused but instead walked confidently over to where she was and kneeled over and prayed over her until she sat up and began to speak again. It wasn't until I heard him pray that I understood that dedication, faithfulness, commitment, and time is what brings grace for power. I didn't know about meditation and prayer. I heard him on his knees for a while but then watched him sitting with his bible on his lap as if he was listening to the words on the pages speaking to him. I had no idea what meditation was and frankly didn't believe my mind could quietly listen to God talk. It had never happened, or so I thought. But what couldn't be argued was the fact that after every one of those special times of prayer, we saw miracles that I didn't see in other places. After a few of those all night prayer meetings, my bible became clearer, and I could understand better. Excitement began to build as I learned more about how the Holy Spirit took course. After learning more about Him, I wanted to know more. The more time I gave, the more He blessed; however, I soon learned the less I gave in worship, time, and prayer the more I missed and then desired His presence.

Moving forward, shortly after beginning my first pastorate, I was invited to a "Camp Meeting" service. I had heard of the minister and that he was an excellent teacher. As I sat, I could tell it was going to be a special night. After his message, he appeared to be ready to retire and close the service. However, on the way to the office he paused to notice a lady on the second row. He then asked for a chair to be set slightly in front of the others and asked if she didn't mind taking this seat. To my surprise, she stood and walked with a limp. I thought, "What a terrible thing to do to embarrass her." He reached down gently and placed his hand on the back of her ankle. I was seated to her right on the front row and was amazed at what I witnessed. It appeared as if her leg grew in his hands. He then asked her to please stand. I said to the pastor, "Does he know her? Is this real?" The pastor said, "It's not possible he knows who she is!" When she stood, both legs were the same length! Another miracle before my eyes! THIS TIME I WASN'T GONNA QUIT WITHOUT ANSWERS! The small little southern town known as Greenville didn't have many good hotels, so I went to the one I thought was the best and waited. After a while, the evangelist, Dave Roberson, came along. I introduced myself and asked if he'd pardon the intrusion, but there is a place in God that you know, and my soul is tired of crying for it (Matthew 5:6). Having had a season of rejection and church politics, I only wanted to know how to be close enough to our Lord where he would find grace enough to use me. Much to my surprise, he invited me to walk with him. From about 11 p.m. to 3 a.m. he sat in the chair in his room and me on the floor as he mentored me on Romans 8!! The talk for the evening was "the walk in the spirit, the walk of power." I wept so much at truth it was difficult to drive back to Rocky Mount safely. To finally know, *"There is therefore now no condemnation to them which are in Christ Jesus, who walk not after the flesh, but after the Spirit"* (Romans 8:1 KJV).

I knew about church history. From Topeka to Houston, to California, from Bonnie Brae to Azusa Street, the names of Frank Bartleman, William Seymour, Charles Parham, and hundreds of others who paid the price of commitment with prayer and fasting that the glory of the Only begotten of the Father would descend among His creation.

Globally, the 70's, 80's, and 90's were a time we saw the grace of God in so many different manifestations. Success, nice churches, prosperous pastors, and prosperous pews all made us know God is good. It almost seemed like a time where we duplicated the behavior of David. Good doctors and free legal advice from our treasured newest members let us know we were in good hands. With such large numbers, it seemed easy to believe we were ok, and hardly anymore did we hear about those prayer meetings that introduced His glory to us. Even if we did, we had other commitments.

Much like Israel we've been working on Mount Gibeon, while God has been trying to get to ZION, doing the priestly duties, while the ark is missing. The miracles have decreased. The seeking is at a minimal. Poverty is creeping back. Racism feels it's ok to come out of the closet, and we are hopeful for government and legislation to fix what the absence of seeking has allowed. Should I even mention the word PANDEMIC?

We recently had a national election. It was one that became very contentious. I was asked about my politics and which candidate I would choose. Even though I felt I was about to be verbally attacked, I responded anyway. The person immediately rebuked me and called my salvation into question because he was pro-life and didn't understand why I would make such a choice. I asked if he'd heard of George Floyd, or Briana Tylor, or Trayvon Martin? He responded, "Yes but what does that have to do with this?" My response was "EVERYTHING!!" I asked would he be willing to count to 520 with me. He said he saw no reason why he should. I responded 520 was 8 minutes and 40 seconds in which I watched a man with a knee on the neck of one of God's creations, and there was no need to call for help because the help was the assistants, while dressed to protect, they only watched. And we watched through the media and were helpless as life left his body. We had to announce BLACK LIVES MATTER just to be understood that there is a difference in being pro-life and PRO-BIRTH! Pro-life means you care all the way until our savior calls them home. You care about the schools of their children and the living condition of the elderly, equal justice under the law. You won't give an order to gas protestors and take a picture with a borrowed bible in 20 minutes while allowing over 5 hours of insurrection on the Capitol and say nothing and leave five souls dead! God establishes His word and intends for us to be clear about our choices.

David has proved that the will of the majority is not always the will of God. A good idea is not necessarily a God idea. The music won't move Him and anointing the unsanctified won't change him. Making an attempt to move the presence of God contrary to direction or allowing passion to inspire without preparation can prove to be fatal. David was now seeking spiritual opinions from self-guided, self-appointed, untrained spiritual individuals with passions that led them to a frontline procession that wounded the very heart of God' who had rescued many of them also in the wilderness and was bringing them to a wealthy place of promise.

Just a little over 100 years ago, the Holy Spirit was poured out on Azusa Street, and the ark was coming down the streets of time to destiny. How inspiring to think we would see healings like our Lord did. The blind could see, and the sick healed. Peace in communities with miracles in churches. All could have the same hope that grace would rest in this house too, but now it seems the old has reared its ugly head again.

It seems our days have become busy and our alters empty. It's risky to share your challenges with those who say I'll pray for you while you remain uncertain about their agenda for fear it will not be the safe place you'd hoped. It seems our conversations have become debates, and you must choose sides to feel safe. There is a feeling across the country that suggests we have become tribal. That perhaps, I'm against you if we are not part of the same group or if I disagree with you on the interpretation of any scripture. I revisited the text, *'nation shall rise against nation'* and wondered would that include denomination or also imagination? All of us want to enjoy the benefits of having others believe in us and even, if necessary, speak a word of encouragement for us. But is it done blindly as David did and chose an allegiance that becomes disobedient to Jehovah's word and creates hindrances to the move of the Holy Spirit? But now, **THE ARK HAS TURNED ASIDE!**

Chapter 4
The Education of Passion

My wife has a little saying that is voiced from time to time. If there should come a time when there is a matter of discussion, no matter what the subject and I feel I've heard her and she's heard me, perhaps even the topic has been exhausted, I simply get quiet. The reason to me is quite simple. There's nothing else to say. After a reasonable space of time, when she pauses from her Zoom calls or I mentally return from being immersed in research, she will softly make her presence known and say, "Your silence is very loud!" We both chuckle and then return to our norm.

The point should not be wasted on us that here we find a great deal of loud, silent communication. It is true that Saul inquired not about the glory of God, but it is also true that David inquired not about the process. It is not mentioned that God called out to Saul about the ark, neither is it mentioned that he stopped David and shouted out to Uzzah. Loud silence may be an invitation to research our activities and be certain we have not engaged in selfish, narcissistic approval.

How did we return again to the Saul's of our day? When did it become ok to have a form of Godliness but deny the power thereof? (2 Timothy 3:5). What would be the inspiration to desire Mount Gibeon with no glory, miracles, signs, or wonders when Mount Zion is in view? Is it possible to trust those who say "I love you" with one hand but have the spirit of Saul and a spear in the other? While we are constantly losing those we love to cancers and other dreadful diseases, this should not be the time for us to discontinue our press towards the mark of the high call (Philippians 3:14). It should be abundantly clear to all that in times past, God did choose to exercise his anger. It makes you wonder just how close David was to hearing the words Jehovah spoke to Moses in Exodus 32, "*Now therefore let me alone, that my wrath may wax hot against them, and that I may consume them: and I will make of thee a great nation.*"

Clearly, David was upset by the death of Uzzah and memorialized the location by naming it so "Perez-uzzah." "*And David was displeased, because the LORD had made a breach upon Uzzah: and he called the name of the place Perez-uzzah to this day.*" This was the very wrong response to the death of Uzzah. David was upset <u>with God</u> but not with Uzzah. Scripture does not say David was displeased with Uzzah, who touched the Ark, but it was because God touched Uzzah. So, it is God who gets criticized because of tragedy. That tone has a familiar ring to it. It sounds a lot like Adam, "*And the man said, the woman whom thou gavest to be with me, she gave me of the tree, and I did eat*" (Genesis 3:12

KJV). How typical it is of man who was walking outside of the will of God. When we do things our way instead of God's way, we end up criticizing the right way rather than condemning the wrong way.

I would think that David, however, is engulfed with many different emotions. Feeling the passion to bring the glory of God to where all people can worship must have created within him a feeling of some level of holiness. After all, the Ark had been in the care of the family of Abinadab for almost 100 years. It is not hard to conceive from David's position that Uzzah and Ahio, having been familiar with the Ark throughout their entire life, if there were any breach or disobedience present, they would have known. After all, they were raised with the Ark, which represented the very seat of God. Surely, they have not been this close to the glory all these years without learning the do order of God's desire. But such was not the case. Here what the book of Job says, "*Great men are not always wise: neither do the aged understand judgment*" *(*Job 32:9 KJV).

During the year 2020, we had to respond to the Covid 19 virus. Churches, businesses, schools and so many other areas were affected in ways none would have expected. I have always had a love for music and really had a desire for the bass guitar. So, with a little more time on my hands than I had planned, I thought it a good idea to learn how to make good music. I went online and saw one that looked good, and next thing you know, it was at my door. I took it out the box, plugged it into the amp, and what came next was so disappointing. The strings were different sizes and made different notes. It wasn't the same as playing my 'air guitar.' Quickly I learned having **passion for something doesn't qualify you, and desire by itself is not enough.** Without proper instruction, you can never achieve the desired goal!

David is now having an emotion he's not familiar with. Heretofore, all of his life, his passion has proved to be his light and the pointer for his direction. I am certain David has vivid memories of Samuel requesting his presence while he was out with the sheep. Clearly, he remembers being anointed in front of his brothers. Passion led him to kill a lion and a bear that he would not be a failure in the assignment given him by his father. Passionately, David played for the King who was simultaneously trying to destroy him with his spear. Passion also led him only to remove part of the King's skirt and not to take Saul's life. With all of the victories that have been manifested for the shepherd boy, from his covenant keeping God, "How is it possible that Uzzah's death was because of me? Has my passion betrayed me?" It is a fact when God chastens us, we need to receive the chastening in the spirit of meekness lest we add sin to sin. Here David adds sin to sin because he did not react well at all to the chastening of God. Instead of frowning at God, he should have fallen on his knees before God. *"Despise not the chastening of the Lord"*

(Proverbs 3:11). In verse 9, David's fear of the Lord is made clear. David was now afraid that the judgment that came upon Uzzah could come upon him. This is not the fear that is synonymous with reverence and respect. This is a fear that views God in an unloving and dishonoring way. It is the fear of the unrepented who fears the judgment of God upon his evil. Many live a life of fear. Since they will not fear God in a way that speaks of reverence and respect, they often will doubt his love and speak of dread and dismay. Since they will not fear God to the extent that they obey him, they will fear him for the judgment that comes upon disobedience. Terror, not tranquility, is the experience of the unrepentant.

Much has happened in David's life since he was summoned from his shepherd duties to be anointed by Samuel as Israel's next King. David had gone through a number of very challenging experiences, which explained his boldness and prepared him for his duties to be King of Israel. Whenever God calls us to honorable, privilege, and important duties, you can be sure that he will give us much training for the task. That training may take years and be very difficult at times, but God does not put anyone into a position of great responsibility without ample preparation. Sometimes when we become aware that we are chosen for an important task, our ego becomes inflated. But that inflated ego, which will hinder our performance and is ignorant of our call, will be deflated in God's school of preparation: a school that replaces inability with ability, foolish with wisdom, immaturity with maturity, and carnality with spirituality.

If your place in life is currently a desolate place, be careful that you do not look only at the circumstances before you move. Make sure you have God's orders before moving. It may be hard to stay and wait for instruction, but before moving, you must have God's order, or the move will prove to be worse than the time you spent waiting.

The will of God was revealed to David a step at a time. We do not learn everything all at once. We go to school for a number of years because our learning experience is a step at a time. So it is with the will of God. The revelation of the will of God comes to us generally a step at a time. We will, however, always know enough to guide us out of our present condition. Leading us a step at a time helps to keep our eyes fixed upon God and helps to promote our faith. But it is hard on the flesh, and those who live by the flesh rather than by faith will not do well in learning the will of God.

Persistence in learning the will of God has much to do with progress in learning the will of God. The will of God is insight and great knowledge, and God does not give it to those who do not value it. Had David not persisted in learning the will of God, he would have come up short in his knowledge of God, and this leads to incomplete obedience and frustration. Therefore, how important it is to persist in discovering his only will. Those who do not value it will not be very successful in learning. But until you prove your value of the will of God by continually pursuing the knowledge of him, you will not learn much about him or what's next.

Also, this educated passion would prove to benefit David's followers. Some not only would be elevated from being once known as fugitives, but now with David's godly ascension, they will be holding high posts in government. How important is it to obey the will of God, for it is the key to blessing those around us who also submit to His vision and leadership? David's followers will now be given high posts of service in his monarchy. In like manner, those who faithfully follow Christ now when he is rejected will be honored by him when he comes into his glory. Paul summed up this truth when he said, *"If we suffer, we should also reign with him; If we deny him, he also will deny us"* (2 Timothy 2:12).

This experience of David foreshadowed the experience of the nation of Israel regarding Jesus (who is typified by the ark). Israel was disobedient regarding Christ (they rejected him as Messiah). So, the blessing went to the Gentiles instead *"Then Paul and Barnabas waxed bold, and said, it was necessary that the word of God should first have been spoken to you: but seeing ye put it from you, and judge yourselves unworthy of everlasting life, lo, we turn to the Gentiles"* (Acts 13:46 KJV).

With all of the good that our passion leads us to, there are several ways that our passions can expose us. Personal impulse and unchecked ambitions can obtain a false freedom, and without the education needed to perform the expected task, can cause roadblocks. Without wisdom and valued instructions, our passions will lead us to selfish agendas and place us on the defense.

Rowan Williams, in his writings *Being Human*, says this, *"If I had to try to sum up what the word 'passion' means in the classical Christian tradition it seems to me to designate two things: the uncritical affirmation of the ego, and the positioning of that ego in a state of struggle and rivalry."*

Whether angry, embarrassed, or uncertain, possibly all three, David nevertheless retreated in a loud silence for the space of three months. It is a difficult thing to be wrong in front of 30,000 of your followers. And yet, the authenticity of his call and the strong pull of his destiny leaned on his passion. David provided a sterling lesson for us all. He had suffered his way to the top. No love from father, brothers, or king; I believe he learned at some point it's possible to learn to forgive yourself, and simply realize I made a mistake. *"But the God of all grace, who hath called us unto his eternal glory by Christ Jesus, after that ye have suffered a while, make you perfect, stablish, strengthen, settle you."* (1 Peter 5:10).

David was successful in sounding an alarm to his people. He was successful in causing them to think we can be better than the ones before us. He was correct in believing the mark of Ichabod is still upon us, and the glory has not yet been restored. His passion clearly propelled him to bring the glory (that he'd never seen or known) back to the people of God. As previously discussed, the Ark was taken by the Philistines during the Prophet Eli's watch. David never knew what a wonderful sight it was to witness the glory of God rising between the cherubs and to be welcomed into the eternal God's presence. Passion can cause you to believe that the impossible is possible, and that you can succeed where others have failed. However, the tension in your passion on some occasions can be very unsettling. There is the potential for a bit of duality. While David is very much focused on succeeding in his godly mission, he's also learned that his aggression can also bring disappointment. Passion has unknowingly summonsed David to a seat of transition. He was about to represent our Lord Jesus in a way that could not be articulated to him. David is now wrestling with the unknown feeling of being Prophet, Priest, and King. The desire for God to dwell amongst his people is a priestly function, but the anointing to be King is a political one. In this sea of emotions, he feels the prophetic voice to summons the people to their proper place, which is worship before the only God, Jehovah! This desire in any light would be considered very noble. It is obvious that David had heard of the Ark because he references the abuse of ignoring it: *"And let us bring again the ark of our God to us: for we inquired not at it in the days of Saul" (1 Chronicles 13:3).* While David notes Saul's faults, he appears to be blinded by his own. With all the favor on his life, he never thought to inquire about order and process. **Favor is never a substitute for obedience.** With battle victories and newfound fame, he seemed to think he was exempt from a godly process. *"And the women answered one another as they played, and said, Saul hath slain his thousands, and David his ten thousands" (1 Samuel 18:7).* Sadly, what worked to bring him favor with men, would not work with God. *"It is the glory of God to conceal a thing: but the honor of kings is to search out a matter"* (Proverbs 25:2).

Now that David is King, it appears as if he goes about Royal duties. It's not until he hears that God had chosen to bless the temporary location of the Ark, that he resumed his quest. When David found out that Obed-edom was being blessed because of the possession of the ark, it rekindled David's desire to get the ark into Jerusalem. The blessings of Obed-edom had impressed David, and David wanted to experience the quiet desire that wouldn't go away.

"And it was told king David, saying, The Lord hath blessed the house of Obed-edom, and all that pertaineth unto him, because of the ark of God" (2 Kings 6:12 KJV).

Let us be reminded that the ark was situated in the third realm of the Tabernacle and represented the very presence of God himself. Some call this third dimension the Feast of Tabernacles. Indeed, it was after Passover, then the feast of Pentecost, and finally the realm of God's glory.

As earlier stated, the purposes of God often manifest in threes. When God moved from the Outer Court to the Holy Place, from the Feast of Passover to the Feast of Pentecost, the order changed. The priesthood changed. From the Reformation of the early 1500s to the outpouring at Azusa Street in 1906, men walked in the truth of justification by faith (Martin Luther), water baptism sanctification (John Wesley), and divine healing (A. B. Simpson). But God had more to add with men such as Charles Parham and William Seymour. They opened up this second feast, and each of us are glad for the experience of the Holy Ghost as we honor and deeply appreciate the Pentecostal roots of our fathers and mothers in the Lord. At this point, we emphasize that the greater feast always swallows up and includes all the truth and glory of the previous feast. Pentecost includes Passover, and the current Feast of Tabernacles includes Passover and Pentecost. We cannot do away with the foundation, the underpinning, the first principles. Our passion is to finish the building and hasten the coming of him, who is the capstone! To preach the full gospel is to preach Jesus all the way from the Outer Court to the Most Holy Place. He is savior, baptizer, and King! In Psalm 22, Jesus is the savior; In Psalm 23, the Shepherd; In Psalm 24, the sovereign. He is Jesus, the Christ, our Lord. He is the sum of all.

David has been chosen to be the first representation of what has never been. Never before in the family of God had there been Prophet, Priest, and King. His unusual and unsettling passion undoubtedly needed to be perfectly aligned with the spoken eternal word. Here it is made clear that David researched the order that Jehovah had already set in place. "Then David said, *none ought to carry the ark of God but the Levites: for them hath the Lord chosen to carry the ark of God, and to minister unto him forever. And David gathered all Israel together to Jerusalem, to bring up the ark of the Lord unto his place, which he had prepared for it." "And said unto them, Ye are the chief of the fathers of the Levites: sanctify yourselves, both ye and your brethren, that ye may bring up the ark of the Lord God of Israel unto the place that I have prepared for it. For because ye did it not at the first, the Lord our God made a breach upon us, for that we sought him not after the due order" (1 Chronicles 15:2,3,12,13 KJV)*.

David now gave the Lord his proper place in his plans and submitted to the regulations he had given. He learned from painful experience that God's work must be done in God's prescribed way if his approval and blessing were to rest upon the same. Only those whom God has specifically appointed must carry the sacred Ark. David now realized that suitable preparation must precede holy activities. It would also appear that David recognizes the priestly anointing on his life. It is clear that he recognizes that he must ask the priesthood with the proper information of the scriptures. Anointing the "unsanctified" only leads to disappointment and death. Not only does David have to work on personal transformation, but he also has to make the followers around him better servants with knowledge and humility. He has been chosen to walk a path that has never been seen. So often we look back at the life of David with criticism and judgement but how strong was his passion to be called to write the future, live it loudly, even though he'd never seen the path to bring about destiny.

The real work that must be done to qualify us is always a heart matter. It is obvious David had a change of heart and a lesson in educating his passion: *"Then David said, None ought to carry the ark of God but the Levites... for that we sought him not after the due order"* (1 Chronicles 15:2,13). David's study has now paid off. He confesses his wrong actions, "We sought him not after the due order." *"Blessed art thou O Lord, Teach me thy statutes" (Psalm 119:12 KJV).*

He owned his mistake of moving the ark by a new cart. Clearly, he came to realize nothing would change without doing it God's way. Humility became his strength as he inquired about God's way. Not only was he led, but it was also necessary for the leader to have good and godly instructions for those who trusted and wanted to help and aid in this new order.

*"For at that time day by day there came to David to help him, **until it was a great host, like the host of God**" (1 Chronicles 12:22 KJV).*

David learns how to worship God through his word. He has discovered what pleases God because it was written. It is no longer guesswork through untrained passion or popular demand, it is the exact word of God. He got the right people to carry the ark and ordered them to purify themselves before they carried the ark. Here we now see the calling of the workers and the cleansing of the workers. Only the Levites were appointed to do this job. That did not make them better, but it just made them the only ones called for this assignment. Then David said, "None ought to carry the ark of God but the Levites: for them hath the Lord chosen to carry the ark of God, and to minister unto him forever." *"And said unto them, Ye are the chief of the fathers of the Levites: sanctify yourselves, both ye and your brethren, that ye may bring up the ark of the* LORD *God of Israel unto the place that I have prepared for it"* *"So the priests and the Levites sanctified themselves to bring up the ark of the* LORD *God of Israel"* (1 Chronicles 15:14 KJV).

During this second attempt, David also prepared singers. David **prepared** a great choir and musicians to sing praise unto God. *"And David spake to the chief of the Levites to appoint their brethren to be the singers with instruments of musick, psalteries and harps and cymbals, sounding, by lifting up the voice with joy"* (1 Chronicles 15:16 KJV).

"And it was told king David, saying, The Lord hath blessed the house of Obed-edom, and all that pertaineth unto him, because of the ark of God. So David went and brought up the

ark of God from the house of Obed-edom into the city of David with gladness. And it was so, that when they that bare the ark of the Lord had gone six paces, he sacrificed oxen and fatlings. And David danced before the Lord with all his might; and David was girded with a linen ephod. So David and all the house of Israel brought up the ark of the Lord with shouting, and with the sound of the trumpet" (2 Samuel 6:12-15 KJV).

The day has finally come. The lessons to be learned about the due order of God have been realized. The procession from the house of Obed-edom up the road roughly about 10 miles to Jerusalem has finally happened. Passion has been educated by wisdom, order has been restored with respect, the shadow of failure and the term Ichabod has been removed, and the ark is now pleased to dwell with the family of God.

Chapter 5
Things Have Been Changed

During the three months which the ark of God was in the house of Obed-edom, David saw that the blessings of God came upon that household. He gave himself to seeking the Lord and searching his word, and it is certain that God gave him understanding and insight into his will.

David now prepares a place for the ark of the Lord. There is no doubt that David pitched the Tabernacle by the leading of God. It may be questioned whether David was in the will of God setting up another Tabernacle when the Tabernacle of Moses was already in existence.

A brief review of the previous events concerning those who touched the ark of God with unsanctified hands, whether they were the Philistines or Israelites, lets us know that none should dare to presume an unlawful action concerning the ark.

If David dared to presume to set up another Tabernacle in opposition to or contradiction of the Tabernacle of Moses, he also would have been struck dead. Even as death and plagues have judged many. From the death of Hophni and Phineas when the ark was taken out of the Tabernacle at

Shiloh, to the first bringing up of the ark of God by David, death, and judgment have prevailed. So, if David was out of the will of God and establishing another Tabernacle, he certainly would have been judged too by God. David was indeed in the will of God, as the scriptures show.

"And when he had removed him, he raised up unto them David to be their king; to whom also he gave testimony, and said, I have found David the son of Jesse, a man after mine own heart, which shall fulfil all my will" (Acts 13:22 KJV).

The Tabernacle of Moses was the place of God at first. Now the Tabernacle of David becomes the place prepared for God. God always desires a place to dwell with his people. David prepared a place for the ark of God.

*"And they brought in the ark of the Lord, and set it **in his place**, in the midst of the tabernacle that David had pitched for it"* (2 Samuel 6:17 KJV).

In carefully noting the scriptures, we conclude the Tabernacle of David was pitched in Mount Zion, and Zion is called the city of David. Here David placed the company of priests and Levites who have been taken from the "old order" that they had known for years as in Moses Tabernacle. In David's Tabernacle, these priests came into a "new order" as pertaining to worship. It should be noted that transitioning into a new revelation can be very difficult. Many individuals have missed being baptized into the timing of God because they couldn't let go of the old and embrace the new. The memory of past glory can sometimes paralyze the process of bringing us into a new and present reality of God's will. It's not just present in our times; Ezra also experienced the same challenge as the people returned from Babylon. There was a mixing of faith. The old order and new were located in the same place, both challenged. Old wanted what they remembered, and new with a desire of what could be. This dilemma is not new, memory verses destiny: *"And when the builders laid the foundation of the temple of the Lord, they set the priests in their apparel with trumpets, and the Levites the sons of Asaph with cymbals, to praise the Lord, after the ordinance of David king of Israel. And they sang together by course in praising and giving thanks unto the Lord; because he is good, for his mercy endureth for ever toward Israel. And all the people shouted with a great shout, when they praised the Lord, because the foundation of the house of the Lord was laid. But many of the priests and Levites and chief of the fathers, who were ancient men, that had seen the first house, when the foundation of this house was laid before their eyes, wept with a loud voice; and many shouted aloud for joy: So that the people could not discern the noise of the shout of joy from the noise of the weeping of the people: for the people shouted with a loud shout, and the noise was heard afar off"* (Ezra 3:10-13 KJV). More times than we would hope, change is a fighting word. Sometimes it's interpreted as if what we did

95

was wrong, rather than what's taking place is an update in the plan of God.

Again, the Tabernacle of David had no outer court with its attendant furniture, and holy places, in contrast to the Tabernacle of Moses at Mount Gibeon.

These priests and Levites simply had the holiest of all, or the most holy place, and in it the ark of the covenant. The obvious question to be asked at this junction is what did God have in mind? What was being foreshadowed?

In Old Testament actuality, David had transferred the Ark of the covenant from the Tabernacle of Moses to the Tabernacle of David. There was simply a transference of the holiest of all. The priests in David's Tabernacle could simply and boldly enter into the most holy place. They had access before the ark of the Lord. There was no standing veil between them and the ark, as there had been for centuries in the Tabernacle of Moses. They had boldness to enter in "within the veil" because the veil belonged to the Tabernacle of Moses, **NOT** to the Tabernacle of David. Let us be clear; **THERE WAS NO VEIL**!

It is not lost that God had given David an unprecedented plan that his glory should be available to all. No longer was his presence restricted to a priest once a year, but now David has unveiled the heart of God to dwell with all of His creation.

Sadly, however, men are oftentimes given to history and tradition. During the rebuilding of Herod's Temple, the veil was reinstalled; however, Jesus removed it <u>again</u> and rent it at his death that we may have access to his glory.

In contrast to the Tabernacle of Moses and the priests at Mount Gibeon, these priests in the Tabernacle of Zion did not offer animal sacrifices. They offered sacrifices of praise, joy, and thanksgiving. He had the ministry of the singers and the musicians both in full operation. They were to offer up "spiritual sacrifices" in Mount Zion in the Tabernacle of David.

Mount Zion was the city of David the King. It was the original Hill of the Jebusites. The territory was given to the tribe of Benjamin as part of their inheritance (Joshua 18:28). However, the Jebusites never lost the Citadel, for they held it or part of it until the time of David. Zion was captured during the time of King David. After he captured it, the stronghold of Zion became known as the city of David.

There are two dominant themes associated with Zion in both testaments, that which is political and that which is religious.

Zion - The city of King David, the capital city, the governing city of the nation, sets forth the governmental or political aspect of Zion.

Zion - The city of the Tabernacle of David, the sacred city, the religious capital of the nation, sets forth the spiritual or ecclesiastical aspect of Zion.

In bringing these two aspects together, Zion is seen as the political and ecclesiastical city of the nation Israel. Here King

David ruled and reigned over the people of the Lord. Here the government of God was revealed in the Kingdom of David, and the Kingdom of God in the chosen nation.

It was also here that David led the nation in the order of worship and established in his Tabernacle. Here the worship of God was seen and heard, as the musicians and singers functioned in their proper courses.

Thus, Zion combines in itself the political and religious unity of the nation, and King David exemplifies the ministry of a King and priest unto God.

The typical truth becomes evident in the light of the New Testament revelation. Jesus Christ, the greater son of David, is King in Zion, the city of God. He rules and reigns. His government is revealed. He is King of kings and Lord of lords (Isaiah 9:6-9; Revelation 19:16).

He is also priest. He leads the host of the redeemed, the true Israel of God, in worship to the father (Hebrews 2:12); (Psalms 22:22). He is King-Priest after the order of Melchizedek, (Hebrews 7:1) combining in himself the governmental and spiritual administrations over the people of God.

The Lord Jesus Christ is the savior in Zion. *"And it shall come to pass that whosoever shall call in the name of the Lord shall be saved" (Acts 2:21). "For in Mount Zion an in Jerusalem shall be deliverance" (Joel 2:32 KJV).*

"Rejoice greatly, O daughter of Zion; Shout, O daughter of Jerusalem: Behold, thy King cometh unto thee: He is just, and

having salvation; Lowly, and riding upon an ass, And upon a colt the foal of an ass" (Zechariah 9:9 KJV). See also (Matthew 21:4,5). The great tragedy was seen in the fact that Jesus Christ came to earthly Zion, and his ministry there fulfilled actually many of the Old Testament prophecies concerning earthly Zion, but earthly Zion rejected him. They crucified their King of Zion.

It should be evident to the thoughtful that the fullness of truth cannot possibly apply just to the small geographical hill of Mount Zion. Indeed, that was simply the earthly, the geographical, the natural place, but it pointed to the heavenly, the spiritual, and that place which is eternal. And this also is so, the earthly Zion with its kingly and priestly functions, its sorrows and joys, its defeats and triumphs, and its worship, all shadow the heavenly and spiritual Zion.

Let us consider some New Testament truths about Zion. Here we have apostolic interpretation and application of some of these verses from the Old Testament. *"As it is written, Behold, I lay in Sion a stumblingstone and rock of offence: and whosoever believeth on him shall not be ashamed"* (Romans 9:33) (1 Peter 2:6-8). Here the Apostle Paul tells how the Jewish nation, as a whole, stumbled over Christ Jesus, the foundation stone in Zion. He is the stumbling stone and rock of offense to Jewry. *"And so all Israel shall be saved: as it is written, There shall come out of Sion the Deliverer, and shall turn away ungodliness from Jacob"* (Romans 11:26 KJV).

This is quoted from Isaiah 59: 20. It confirms once again that Jesus Christ is the deliverer out of Zion. He is the only one through whom Israel can be saved. *"But ye are come unto mount Sion, and unto the city of the living God, the heavenly Jerusalem, and to an innumerable company of angels"* **(Hebrews 12:22 KJV).** The writer in Hebrews here encourages the believers concerning the true and heavenly Jerusalem and Zion. Leaving the earthly temple, the animal sacrifices, the Aaronic priesthood, earthly Zion, and Jerusalem, they come to a spiritual temple, to spiritual sacrifices, to the priesthood of Melchizedek and heavenly Zion and Jerusalem.

The whole epistle of Hebrews sets forth the contrast between that which is natural and spiritual, that which is earthly and heavenly, that which is temporal and eternal. Hence, spiritual Zion and Jerusalem are certainly greater than the earthly Zion and Jerusalem, for the first was only a type of the one to come. *"Wherefore also it is contained in the scripture, behold, I lay in Zion a chief cornerstone, elect, precious, and he that believeth on him shall not be confounded"* (1 Peter 2:6 KJV). This verse is quoted from Isaiah 28:16 and finds its fulfillment in the Lord Jesus Christ as being the foundation stone in his church. *"And I looked, and low, a lamb stood on the Mount Zion, and with him 144 thousand, having his father's name written in their foreheads"* (Revelation 14:1 KJV).

This is the final distinct reference to Zion in the New Testament. A consideration of the verse certainly shows that the Lamb of God does not stand on literal or earthly Mount Zion in Palestine. That was where the lamb was slain. The Mount Zion he stands in is the spiritual and heavenly Zion.

Thus, we have three aspects of the significance of Zion and scriptures. The original in heaven, the type in the Old Testament, and the antitype in the church. God indeed has the true, the heavenly, and the spiritual Zion in mind. Many of the scriptures become meaningless if applied to the geographical location in the Middle East. The eternal Zion is the New Testament reality of the Old Testament shadow. It finds its glorious fulfillment in Christ and his church. The New Testament writers are the infallible interpreters of the Old Testament prophets. They give us the "key" to the significance of Zion. It is impossible to disassociate the Tabernacle of David from the significance of Zion.

Chapter 6
The Returning Glory

It is comforting and reassuring to know that God has a plan. It is not something with trial and error. It was established before the beginning. If we were to take a look at Genesis 1 and then gaze over to John 1, we could see the work of him from the beginning, and then echoed and explained clearly. Sometimes, however, while we are working, things appear a little muddled and often ambiguous on the road to destiny because of assumption or presumption concerning his plan. Unity, however, whether it be with his spirit, his plan, or others chosen is the essential magnet and assuring barometer for success. This is a prerequisite as we noticed that God only blessed David when he aligned himself with the preordained plan. Much like those who came to David to anoint him King, believers today would do well to follow their example.

"All these men of war, that could keep rank, came with a perfect heart to Hebron, to make David king over all Israel: and all the rest also of Israel were of one heart to make David king" (1 Chronicles 12:38 KJV). This is a perfect picture and type of believers following Christ in his Kingdom. A wonderful look, and a glorious foretelling of John's vision in the

Revelation. *"After this I beheld, and, lo, a great multitude, which no man could number, of all nations, and kindreds, and people, and tongues, stood before the throne, and before the Lamb, clothed with white robes, and palms in their hands;* [10] *And cried with a loud voice, saying, Salvation to our God which sitteth upon the throne, and unto the Lamb" (Revelation 7:9,10 KJV).*

Beyond any doubt, it is the will of the father to manifest his glory as it is recorded in the scripture (Habakkuk. 2:14). Yet Paul admonishes us that things must be decent and in order (1 Corinthians 14:40) as the believers learned in the book of Acts to be in one place but greater than that, on one accord (Acts 2:1).

The mysteries of God remain that, however, on many occasions, he has chosen to reveal and remove some from behind the veil. The mysteries can be discerned and interpreted through obedience, diligence, sanctification, and research. It is the father's pleasure to dwell with his family, and as Omega, his plan we've heard our Lord say on the cross is finished. As we have heard the story of David in 2 Samuel 9:1 concerning the invitation of Jonathan's son Mephibosheth to a table that has already been set, so too are we reminded by Paul that we have been made to sit together with Christ in heavenly places (Ephesians.2:6). As Kings and priests, it's not a very good look to behave as complainers and beggars. I am eternally optimistic that the plan of God

103

remains unscathed and is positioned to be launched through the faith of a chosen generation, a Royal priesthood, and peculiar people. It is always his practice to have the end planned from the beginning. Nothing surprises him, and nothing is new to him. Solomon profoundly puts it this way: *"The thing that hath been, it is that which shall be; and that which is done is that which shall be done: and there is no new thing under the sun" (Ecclesiastes 1:9 KJV).*

"That which hath been is now; and that which is to be hath already been; and God requireth that which is past" (Ecclesiastes 3:15 KJV).

Just as Abraham, Moses, and David had been chosen and were obedient in consenting and giving their yes to serve God, we too are a chosen people for a chosen time and the chosen assignment. Nothing is by chance or accident, whether covid or racism, famine or drought, earthquake or disasters, **GOD IS IN CHARGE!** There are no surprises to Him, and we are destined to be strong and do mighty exploits (Daniel 11:32). The end was written from the beginning, and we have been chosen to be participants in the manifestation of his glory and mighty works.

What a privilege and what an honor to be invited to walk with them who are being led by the Holy Spirit to usher in the final finished predestined plan of God. **ALLELUIA!**

"And I saw a new heaven and a new earth: for the first heaven and the first earth were passed away; and there was

no more sea. And I John saw the holy city, new Jerusalem, coming down from God out of heaven, prepared as a bride adorned for her husband. And I heard a great voice out of heaven saying, Behold, the tabernacle of God is with men, and he will dwell with them, and they shall be his people, and God himself shall be with them, and be their God. And God shall wipe away all tears from their eyes; and there shall be no more death, neither sorrow, nor crying, neither shall there be any more pain: for the former things are passed away. And he that sat upon the throne said, Behold, I make all things new. And he said unto me, Write: for these words are true and faithful. And he said unto me, It is done. I am Alpha and Omega, the beginning, and the end. I will give unto him that is athirst of the fountain of the water of life freely. He that overcometh shall inherit all things; and I will be his God, and he shall be my son" (Revelations.21:1-7 KJV).

Bibliography

Brueggeman, W. (2018). *The Prophetic Imagination.*

Fortress Press, Minneapolis, MN.

Caird, G. B. (2002). *The Language and Imagery of the Bible.*

Gerald Duckworth, London.

Donin, Rabbi. H. H. (1972). *To Be a Jew.* Basic Books New

York, NY.

Edersheim, A. (1890). *Old Testament Bible History.* William

B. Eerdmans Publishing, Grand Rapids, MI.

Farrer, A. (1963). *A Rebirth of Image.* Wipf and Stock,

Eugene, OR.

Rashi. (1994). *Exodus.* Mesorah Publications, Brooklyn,

New York.

Richards, E.R. & O'Brien, B.J. (2021). *Misreading Scripture*

with Western Eye. IVP Books. Downers Grove, IL.

Varner, K. (1991). *The Priesthood is Changing.* Destiny

Image, Shippensburg, PA.

Varner, K. (1995). *Whose Right It Is.* Destiny Image,

Shippensburg, PA.

Williams, R. (2018). *Being Human*. Eerdmans Publishing, Grand Rapids, MI.

Wright, N. T. (2011). *Revelation for Everyone*. Westminster John Knox Press, Louisville, KY.

Wright, N.T. (1989). *Broken Signposts*. HarperCollins New York, NY.

Zlotowitz, Rabbi. M. & Scherman, Rabbi N. (2011). *1 Samuel*. Mesorah Publications, Brooklyn, New York.

Zlotowitz, Rabbi. M. & Scherman, Rabbi N. (1987). *1 Chronicles*. Mesorah Publications, Brooklyn, New York.

About the Author

Father, pastor, best-selling author, visionary, counselor, dynamic leader, psychologist, full-time clergyman, grandfather, husband, and an established servant for the world, Dr. Donald A. Wright is a man of great

impact. He is equipped with an insightful capacity of an accurate and deep intuitive understanding of the Kingdom of God and our country's well-being. Dr. Wright is a strategic thinker and pioneer that sees our future from the mountaintop. Being led by wisdom, he steadily and safely gives guidance to those he advises so that they arrive at the intended destination. Anchored in a belief system based on what the Bible says, Dr. Donald A. Wright rightly divides the word of truth and remains a rock-solid shepherd for this world even in times of turbulence, serving as the pastor of The Gathering at Forestville. With precision and clarity, this manservant has imparted wisdom and given direction to the leadership of countless authorities to include some of the most successful administrations of our time on an international, national, and local level. With three earned doctoral degrees in theology, ministry, and psychology; Dr. Wright's genius is not to be understated. With experience, education, and ethical integrity blended with compassion, conviction, commitment to our world, Dr. Donald A. Wright is a kept promise for such a time as this.

When The Ark Turns Aside

The Glory Shall Return

DR. DONALD A. WRIGHT

Made in the USA
Monee, IL
03 December 2021

82872697R00070